Handbook for a
NEW
CONSCIOUSNESS

*the NEXT STEP in
Human Evolution*

* * *

Anton Grosz, PhD

Handbook for a NEW CONSCIOUSNESS
The NEXT STEP in Human Evolution

* * *

Copyright 2025 by Anton Grosz

ISBN 978-0-9717577-5-2

FMA Books,
Newark, Delaware 19702

* * *

All rights reserved. No part of this book may be used or reproduced in any manner whatsoever without written permission of the publisher except in the case of brief quotations embedded in critical articles and reviews.

* * *

Poems are from *Tao of the New Consciousness*, by *The Elder*, (FMA Books, 2018) and are used with permission of the author.

* * *

Cover Design by Danielle Betti

* * *

The true essence of everyone is I AM. This is the message of Anton Grosz. Through his excellent exercises, we evolve in our consciousness, learn that we are all connected, and realize our Oneness. As we learn the deep truth of this message, we discover the deeper meaning of Love, Harmony, Gratitude, and Compassion. I applaud him in his efforts in creating an excellent book that can help humanity to awaken.

Jerry Gin, Chairman, Foundation for Mind-Being Research

* * *

Who am I? Such big questions of life cannot be captured in logical phrases or scientific formulas, they must be experienced. This is the virtue of Anton Grosz's approach. He does not claim that any words of his could bring you enlightenment, but they can persuade you to undertake some experiments, as a result of which you will perceive the world, and yourself, differently. So have fun with your exploration. But know that this may be the first step in the most important journey of your life.

Willis W. Harman, former President of the Institute of Noetic Sciences

Dedication

This book is dedicated to Humanity.

*May it help us rise
to the next level of evolution
and live in peace and harmony
with each other, all living beings,
and the very planet
on which we live.*

Contents

New Consciousness in Seven Key Points viii

Author's Preface x

Part One - Finding the Oneness Within 1
Introduction to New Consciousness 3
Now Is the Time 11
Preparing For Your Journey 15
Say What You Mean Game 18
The Jewel of Truth 20
Please Draw a Tree 25
How Do You Know What You Know? 30
Knowing Game 34
Seeing the Light 43
The New Consciousness Paradigm 55

Part Two - Living the Oneness Within 59
Where Do I Go from Here? 61
New Consciousness Defined 64
Inside - Outside 68
Looking Out/Looking In Game 77
It's All About Balance 83
Meeting I to I 88
Evolution of Me Game 97
Light Upon the Water 104

Part Three - Earth and Evolution 107
Science/Religion and New Consciousness 109
Now The Real Fun Begins 114
The Only Constant is Change 116
There Had to be a First Time 123
Retracing Evolution: The Trek Begins 127
Solid Like a Rock 131
Growing Like a Plant 136
Moving Like an Animal 142
Thinking Like a Human 157
On Beyond Human 163

Part Four - Universe and Creation 165
I AM and the Quantum Connection 167
The Spaceship Experience 172
I Am in Space 175
2D... 3D... 4D...? 179
The Wind/Silk Experience 183
I AM at the Start of the Universe 184
Quantum Physics and Phenomenology 193
Putting It All Together 199

Acknowledgments 208

About the Author 210

* * *

New Consciousness in Seven Key Points
It couldn't be easier. It couldn't be more important.

1. The I AM feeling we each experience – our very consciousness – is the Oneness that fills the entire Universe. Religion calls it God. Science calls it Dark Energy. It exists inside and outside everything, including you, the being currently reading these words!

2. Within the adjectives that make each of us special and unique, the conscious I AM of one person doesn't just *feel* the same as the I AM of another person; it *is* the same I AM. Deep inside, at our very core, we are all connected. We are truly one being.

   we are like leaves on a tree
   many different leaves
   only one tree

3. When you feel the connection to the I AM we all share inside as strongly as you feel the connection to your uniqueness and the physical world we all share outside, you will have taken the next step in human evolution. You will be living in New Consciousness.

4. When you live in New Consciousness and realize the universal I AM connection, you will still be special and unique, but you will no longer use your individual skills, talents, and abilities only for your own benefit but for the greater good of all.

5. When enough people experience New Consciousness and a tipping point is reached, humanity as a whole will have evolved and all life on Earth will change for the better. It will usher in an era of Perpetual Peace and Universal Understanding.

> *how could humanity have come so far*
> *without realizing how far we have*
> *strayed off the path?*

6. Humanity must take this seriously! We are at a critical point in our evolution. If we continue as we are, hurting and killing each other, ruled by selfishness, hatred, and the fear of differences, we will destroy ourselves and, most likely, the planet on which we live.

7. This important evolutionary step is voluntary. We must choose to change and work for the good of all if we want humanity to survive. The decision to live in New Consciousness and continue to exist as a living species is up to each and every one of us.

* * *

Author's Preface

In 1978, when I was thirty-seven years old, I had a Near-Death Experience due to lack of oxygen, going through a tunnel into incredibly bright light and having a personal epiphany that forever changed my understanding of reality. When I was able to breathe again and re-entered my body, I knew that what I had believed to be true up to that point was incomplete. There is more to life than what appears in the physical world. Yes, the world of measurement outside is real, but so is the world of meaning inside, a world that doesn't exist in time and space.

Wanting to know more about what I had experienced while separated from my body, I devoted my life from that point on to learning about experiential consciousness, a scientific study known as phenomenology. I read religious works, ancient mystics, indigenous shamans, and modern gurus, studied cognitive science, quantum physics, and chaos theory, and combined these varied principles into a personal meditative practice. I enrolled in the California Institute of Integral Studies, receiving a PhD in 1995 in Philosophy and the Evolution of Human Consciousness.

Little by little, I got deeper and deeper into a dimension where reality is different, science and religion come together, and quantum physics is not just a theory but an actual experience. I found myself shifting from the old way of feeling separate from everyone else to a new way of feeling connected to the One we all are deep within, the feeling that I call "New Consciousness". And I couldn't help feeling, as more and more pieces fell into place, that everything that had happened to me over the years, the talents I have, the people I've met, the lessons I've learned, all the amazing experiences and insights were not just random happenings. Furthermore, they could not have been meant just for me alone.

Handbook for a New Consciousness is a self-study guide based on over forty-five years of experiential research. It is designed to allow you, the reader, not just to hear me tell of my experiences but to experience New Consciousness for yourself within the privacy and safety of your own mind without having to die to do so.

Using simple exercises, stories, and imaginative mind games, the Handbook allows you to experience universal Oneness, recognize the interconnectedness of all life, trace the conscious evolution of life on Earth, and even experience the I AM consciousness present at the start of the universe.

Designed for the devout believer, the dogmatic atheist and everyone in between, the Handbook validates ancient religious beliefs and the findings of modern science. When enough people experience New Consciousness and realize that we are not separate leaves but really one tree, it will usher in an era of Perpetual Peace and Universal Understanding the way it was originally intended to be.

Welcome aboard and thank you for being a part of the future of humanity.

peace............ag

* * *

Part One:

Finding the Oneness Within

✳ ✳ ✳

On Beyond Human

That's what Dr. Seuss would have called it...
        this evolutionary leap we're about to take

It won't look like much of a change...
    from the outside

               we'll still look like humans...
               from the outside

rock to plant...
    plant to animal...
        animal to human...
           been there... done that

human to where we're going next?
                    Just as big!!!

✳ ✳ ✳

Introduction to New Consciousness

A New Consciousness is currently emerging on Earth that is destined to revolutionize life on our planet. This New Consciousness is not just a subject to talk about or a topic for academic examination and analysis. It is a concept more verb than noun — a way to be, a way to act, and a dynamic way to understand reality that will redefine what we mean when we say the word I for each and every one of us.

You should know, right off the bat, New Consciousness is neither a cult nor a religious movement though it actually compliments all true spiritual paths and lets you get deeper into them. Whatever your religion, whatever your faith, if you're happy with the path you're on, keep your current belief system. New Consciousness does not conflict with it. In fact, the exercises in the Handbook should help you on your personal path and make your faith and understanding even stronger.

New Consciousness is also not a touchy-feely kind of spirituality reeking of crystals and mantras. However, spiritual seekers searching for the intense personal experience such spirituality offers, will comfortably resonate with what is said here. The Handbook's exercises should open wide your path as well.

Although the Handbook does not claim to be a scientific treatise, it is designed for scientists, doubters, logicians, thinkers, rational skeptics, agnostics, and downright atheists who refuse to accept on faith alone what they have not seen with their very own eyes and measured with their very own yardsticks.

If you don't believe in anything but quantum physics and mathematics, simply read the Handbook, play the games, and follow your scientific path. You will experience New Consciousness for yourself through a completely different and equally valid door. All it takes is a mind open enough to ask, "What if?" And if you cannot do that, are you really a scientist?

This book is designed to bridge that gap between energy and spirit and explain New Consciousness in a way that makes sense to the devout believer, the dogmatic atheist, and everyone in between. Going behind words that separate us - words like science, theology, God, consciousness, intellect, and intuition - the Handbook touches the immediate, immanent shared inner I experience that truly makes us One, no matter what we want to call it.

Whether you come out the other end feeling that New Consciousness proves the existence of a force known as Dark Energy filling the universe as stated by quantum physics, or validates your faith in an Almighty God as claimed by religion, really doesn't matter either. The actual answer is both, depending on what you expect the answer to be when you ask the question.

What matters is that when you feel this universal force radiating within, you will experience a different dimension, an understanding of the bigger picture. It will feel like freedom, joy, and control over your life. It will allow you to manifest your highest potential, not only for yourself but for the ultimate good of all. And, if you wish to go all the way back to the beginning, you will both understand and experience the nature and structure of the universe as well.

New Consciousness will change what we believe to be true and real today as much as when humans first learned that Earth was not the center of the universe. When enough of us actually feel and live New Consciousness, it will be as big a step for humanity as when human mind evolved out of animal mind so long ago.

To show you just how far humans have already evolved, this giant evolutionary leap, unlike all previous leaps, is voluntary. New Consciousness will not be force-fed to us. Humans are no longer simple creatures controlled by instinct. We have developed minds and self-awareness and feel and think for ourselves. We are able to choose how we want to interact with the worlds we see around us and hear inside us. Wanting to experience New Consciousness is an individual choice.

Adopting New Consciousness as humanity's understanding of reality and the world we see around us will create amazing scenarios we can hardly conceive of today. Science and religion will agree on how the universe was created, bolstered by irrefutable proof that anyone will be able to experience and reproduce.

New Consciousness will allow us to share experiences across time and space, to understand how evolution progressed from non-aware consciousness through human mind each step of the way. It will add a whole new dimension to our knowledge of who we are and how we got here.

New Consciousness will create an awareness that all beings are truly connected at our very core. We will affirm the fact that we share the same I. We will no longer do what we can to improve ourselves at the expense of others but will live with compassion and practice altruism with the goal of creating good and uplifting all.

New Consciousness will help us understand death. We may still not want to leave loved ones and our life on Earth behind, but we will know that when we die, we do not just disappear into nothingness but are still conscious and aware once we shed the body. We will know this is true no matter what our religious beliefs, or even if we don't have any religious beliefs at all.

New Consciousness is free, painless, and open to all. It is, in a word: evolutionary.

Were this a physical evolution taking place, the emergence of a sixth finger or a new blood type that never existed before, we wouldn't doubt its reality. It would be easy to see with the naked eye or some fancy instrument of technology, and we could observe and measure its evolutionary progress. But New Consciousness, the evolutionary experience we shall examine and share, occurs within our minds.

Most importantly, we shall not just be discussing New Consciousness in the abstract. We shall be experiencing New Consciousness in our very own beings. Through the Handbook's unique exercises and mental games, you will have the opportunity to experience New Consciousness for yourself in the safety and privacy of your own mind.

Of course, I am well aware that no teaching, on its own, can make you experience New Consciousness from the outside in. But, if you really want to learn, the teachings in this book can lead you to the point where you can choose to experience New Consciousness for yourself, from the inside out.

Nothing needs to change in the external world for this awareness to occur - only your view of the world and what you bring to your meeting with that world must change. As a result, it will be possible to experience life in a way that adds new perspective and meaning to how life is commonly viewed today.

Computer-generated 3-D art can serve as a metaphor for how to find New Consciousness. Someone may tell you there is a picture hidden in what appears to be a mere mass of color and abstract pattern, and you may stare and squint and cross your eyes until you get a headache, but the image remains hidden until you actually see it. And when you do, suddenly...

There it is. An epiphany. A knowing. The picture that had been there all along. It was hidden only by the fact that you did not know how to look. Once you see it, you can always go back and see it again. For now, you know how to focus your eyes, or in this case, your I.

The basic sense of Self, the feeling that I am an individual and unique being separate from you has taken eons to evolve on Earth. It has created humanity and is vital in understanding today's highly competitive human society, with its win/lose mentality. Some say this feeling of separateness is the very key to being human.

While a strong sense of self, the sense of a singular ego I is critical in human development, it can be taken to extremes. Too many people think that the particular set of characteristics, attributes, and beliefs that they embody are somehow better or more advanced than someone else's. It goes without saying that this feeling that my I is better than your I has led to all of the wars, oppressions, and personal and societal injustices in human history, whatever the details or particulars of any individual conflict.

It need not be this way, as you will experience. How we define ourselves as individuals, what we mean when we say I, is not a constant that has remained unchanged throughout the course of human history nor is it destined to remain as it is in the future.

In New Consciousness, though we know we all share the same I, the physical, mental, emotional and spiritual attributes that make each of us unique will still remain. We will, however, celebrate our differences, using our individual and separate skills and talents not just for our own individual good but for the greater good. It will be similar to how the separate organs in our body all work together to keep the living body the healthiest and best it can be. One can't help wondering, what do they know that we don't?

Think about it. What if there were eyes on the ends of our fingers? And they looked out and saw the thumb and said:

"You stupid thumb, coming from way over there! Take that! And that! And that!"

And what if the fingers scratched the thumb and made it bleed, and it got all infected and the infection went into the hand and back up into the fingers and they also got infected? Would the fingers have scratched the thumb if they knew they were all connected and hurting another would hurt themselves?

Shouldn't humans be at least as smart as our fingers?

Finally, you should know that I have never ceased to question dogma, sectarianism, or blind assumptions masquerading as truth. I expect the same of you, my friend and reader, in exploring what follows. I ask nothing of you that I have not done myself. We are looking to merge intellect and intuition here and in so doing, generate a new reality that can change your life and the world around you.

Welcome to the next step in human evolution. Enjoy the trip.

* * *

Now Is the Time

Humanity is at a critical point in history where every day, somewhere in the world, someone is doing something absolutely horrifying to someone else, like blowing up a marketplace, shooting diners in a restaurant, driving into crowds of tourists, or setting fire to villages, all for the stupidest of reasons - the color of one's skin, or the language one speaks, or the God that one prays to.

Then the group behind the atrocity announces to the media that they are the ones that did it, bragging about all the pain and suffering they have caused to fellow human beings. "Hey, guys, it was us. We're the ones you should be afraid of." Can you believe it?

Even where mass violence is not the norm, life for many is a touch-and-go affair. Earth's resources are distributed so unequally as to be unimaginably cruel and unfair. Some people have so much more than they need, while others have so much less than the minimum even needed for survival. It is estimated that 1 in 9 people on Earth go to bed hungry every night, while almost 9 million people die of malnutrition every year. How inhumane is that?

Anger is spreading around the globe like a virulent disease. Person against person, tribe against tribe, religion against religion, culture against culture, country against country, race against race. Meanwhile, our weapons of mass destruction keep getting more and more sophisticated. How long can this go on before we destroy ourselves and the planet we live on? It's so hard to believe that all this hatred is so ingrained in a species that some claim was made in the image of God.

Yes, there are good people, people who help others, who stand up to hatred, and who rail against the violence they see in the world around them. But they never seem to get the upper hand. New atrocities pop up in places that yesterday were peaceful, and peaceful protests are easily turned into riots by those who believe that they alone have all the answers.

Meanwhile, the real answers, the ones that could end hatred, increase compassion, and provide solutions to the problems humanity faces, appear either so complex or convoluted that it seems they can never come to pass. We can't get people to agree to stop randomly killing each other, so how are we going to get them to agree on this way of doing things, or this mode of governance, or this humanitarian effort? As a species we are banging our heads against the wall even though it hurts so much to do so.

And if that's not enough, we're destroying the very planet on which we live. Our oceans are filled with plastic garbage, our air is filled with toxic chemicals, nuclear waste lies buried beneath the soil, forests are being destroyed, species are becoming extinct, and the balanced ecology that has nurtured all life from the very beginning is beginning to shudder under climate change. How long can we continue in this direction?

If we are unable to change the way we act, the way we treat each other and our world, and the direction we are going as a species, we are clearly destined to destroy ourselves, our planet, and all the other creatures with whom we share this little corner of the universe. A sad prospect, indeed. But what if?

What if all that were needed to turn humanity's destiny from negative to positive, from hatred to love, from violence to compassion, was one little modification to the way we think? What if one tiny change in how humanity views itself and its relation to others was all that was needed to create a completely different understanding of who we are and how we fit into the world in which we live? Wouldn't that be a wonderful and amazing thing to aim for? Is it possible? Why not?

Humanity has come a long way in our knowledge of the universe. We now look up into the sky with a very different understanding of what is real than our forebears, who thought Earth was the center of everything did only several centuries ago. Yet, we currently live in very similar times.

We, too, are missing a truth as obvious and basic and important for the future of civilization as the one they missed back then.

Just as those souls were trapped in a mindset unable to comprehend a new way of looking at reality, so are we. Unless we are able to make that evolutionary leap to a new way of understanding and experiencing reality, the era of human life may be coming to an end.

And what is the obvious truth we are missing simply because we think we understand what we're looking at? It is simply who we think we are when we say I AM. And just like the last evolutionary leap changed the way we looked at everything, this amazing and incredible New Consciousness is powerful enough to change the world as we know it.

* * *

Preparing For Your Journey

New Consciousness is all about looking at the world around you differently than you have up until now. A few simple suggestions will enhance the process as you move towards feeling your evolutionary connection to the Oneness within.

As you prepare to read, get comfortable and take some deep breaths to slow down. Turn off your cell phone, TV, iPad and all distracting technology. The calmer, more centered, and more peaceful you are, the more aware you will be of your inner experiences, and that, after all, is the whole point - becoming aware of your inner self, your consciousness.

The Handbook contains games and exercises that require you to stop reading for a while and look "around," "inside," or both. Take the time. Play the games. This is why these consciousness games have been created. Playing them offers a much better chance of achieving the desired breakthrough into New Consciousness than merely reading about it.

It is also a good idea to simply experience what's happening as it's happening, in as much detail as possible. Try not to pass judgment on any new experiences while in the process. There will be time for critical analysis later, when you slip back into your usual conscious state. "Now" is when you are gathering the information central to that analysis. "Here" is where you are experiencing a new and equally valid way of experiencing reality, doing what is known in anthropological circles as "going native".

However, don't blindly believe my experiences...

... them for yourself.

And remember, an important key to making progress in experiential knowing is affirming what you know to be true the moment you first know it. Stop to let the new experience sink in. Then stop again to recognize that it has sunk in. This can be done by simply saying out loud, "Yes. I now know such and such ..." or writing down what you've learned so you can reaffirm it later. This keeps you from having to repeat the same knowing experience again and again because you can't remember whether you have already gotten it or not.

The challenge is not how fast you can read the Handbook but how well you can actually experience what is presented here. The key is Self-awareness.

Be open to new ideas that can build on what you already know and believe in. Be willing to try them out for yourself, in the safety and privacy of your own mind. It is important to know that there is no right way and no wrong way to go after New Consciousness. Some ways may be straighter than others, or faster, or easier. But whichever way you choose, that's the right way for you. The only wrong way, by the way, is not to go after it at all.

And never forget that new ways of looking at things are not dangerous. The only person you have to fear is the one who says "My way is the only way."

The Handbook is not just about New Consciousness; it *is* New Consciousness. It is designed to lead each individual I to the I AM within us all. That means getting behind the words and into the actual experience. Reading about something means putting it into words. And once you put an experience into words, you are thinking about it, which is something completely different from experiencing it. This is what we are going to explore.

"The path is blocked by vowels and consonants," said the Buddhist monk Khana over a thousand years ago. Trust me, this is still true today, and you can prove it for yourself by playing the, "Say What You Mean Game".

* * *

Say What You Mean Game

Draw something very basic such as a star, a dog, or a house. Now, without showing anyone the picture you drew, ask several of your friends, family members, or co-workers to draw a picture of the same object. Now compare results.

Even after discounting artistic ability, what are the chances that all the drawings will be identical? For "star" someone may draw a five-pointed star, another an asterisk, another a shooting star, another a sheriff's badge. There will be big dogs and little dogs of all shapes and breeds, maybe even a hot dog, while houses can range from single-family homes to apartment buildings, exteriors to floor plans. Someone once drew a hole in a tree to represent a bird's house.

It is not that you communicated what you wanted poorly or that the people you asked were unintelligent or not paying attention. It's just that words are not the reality. They only represent reality as perceived by each individual, and as such, they represent different things to different people.

Using words and expecting people to be in complete agreement on their meanings is unrealistic.

* * *

* * *

Humans don't eat each other anymore...
cannibalism is a thing of the past.
My, my, my...
just look how far we have evolved.

Humans still murder and harm each other...
terrorism is a thing of the present.
My, my, my...
just look how far we still must evolve.

* * *

The Jewel of Truth

Part One

Once upon a time, there was a circular forest with trees, bushes, flowers, and greenery. It was just like any other forest, except that this forest was absolutely, completely, and perfectly round.

Right in the middle of the forest, there was a castle. In the middle of the castle, there was a strong room. In the middle of the strong room, there was a treasure chest. In the middle of the treasure chest, there was a jewel - a beautiful jewel, a special jewel. It was, in fact, the Jewel of Truth.

Over time, lots of people, having heard about the Jewel of Truth, went into the forest to look for it. Some of them went in from over here, some went in from over there, some from way around on the other side. Since it was a circular forest, the distance from the outside to the center and the Jewel of Truth was the same no matter where people entered the forest. But, of course, you have already figured that out.

Now just because you could get to the Jewel of Truth from anywhere on the outside of the forest doesn't mean that everyone who went inside looking for it found it. Some people got tired before they reached it and gave up, some lost their sense of direction along the way and kept going round and round in circles, and some people were lured away by other things that they decided were more interesting.

On the other hand, some people who were traveling through the forest for other reasons, not even looking for the Jewel of Truth, just happened to end up in the right place and find it. Go figure. The important point is that over time, many people found the Jewel of Truth, and from many different directions.

Oh, one of the things I forgot to tell you about the Jewel of Truth and one of the things that makes it so special, is that if you do make your way through the forest, into the castle, into the strong room, into the treasure chest, and touch the Jewel of Truth, not only will you have it with you forever, it will remain there in the treasure chest. In other words, even though you have it, it's always there for someone else to touch as well. Don't ask me how it does that, that's just how it is with the Jewel of Truth.

*** * * ***

Now before you read the rest of the story, take a moment to stop, go inside, and feel yourself going through a forest to look for the castle and the Jewel of Truth. It may seem like a silly thing to have to do, but it really is important that you experience what you read here instead of just hearing me tell you a story. It's the difference between knowing something and knowing about something.

By the way, it doesn't matter what kind of forest or trees it turns out to be, or even if it's a cartoon forest and you're some Pixar prince or princess. Your forest, your castle, your vision. Nobody should tell you what pictures you should see in your very own mind.

And now, back to our story.

* * *

Part Two

So, here's how the problem started. A number of years ago, some people who had never even entered the forest heard about a guy who had made it all the way into the center and touched the Jewel of Truth. Rather than actually going in to look for it themselves, they started putting up signs saying, "This way to the Jewel of Truth."

They cleared out a bunch of trees and made a path partway into the forest along the route they figured the guy had taken. They stayed on the outside of the forest and just kept stopping others, getting in their faces, and saying, "This is the way, this is the way, this is the way to the Jewel of Truth."

"That's cool about your guy", the others would say, "but I want to go into the forest and look for it that way." They would point to somewhere else on the outside of the forest other than the path with the signs.

"No," the people with the signs would say, "you can't. My guy went in this way and he found it. This is the only way to go." And the others would say, "Yeah, I know he went in that way and made it, but other folks went in other ways and they found it too."

The people with the signs would get angrier and angrier and louder and louder, and the more they yelled and fought with the ones who wanted to go in a different way, the more you knew that they had never made it to the center and touched the Jewel of Truth themselves. Because if they had, they'd know you can get to it from anywhere around the outside of the forest, not just that one place and on that one path. It is a circular forest after all.

It got so bad they even started killing people who wanted to take different paths. Can you believe it? Killing people all in the name of the right way to get to the Jewel of Truth. They even killed some people who were on the path they said was the right one but who were saying different words while they walked. Unbelievable!

Meanwhile, that guy in whose name this was all taking place sat there in eternity shaking his head and wondering how his followers could have gotten it so wrong.

So never forget, there are many ways to get into the center of the forest and touch the Jewel of Truth. Follow the guy with all the signs if you want, or follow some person with fewer signs, or someone without any signs, or strike out on your own and blaze your own trail. It doesn't matter. Any approach can work if you truly want to get there and don't give up.

Stay focused and don't worry. When you finally touch the Jewel of Truth you'll know it. And you'll recognize other people who have touched it and know it, too. You'll talk to them and sit with them in a circle around a campfire, just like we're doing here. You'll tell them your story and listen to theirs and you'll marvel at all the different ways that can lead to the Jewel of Truth.

Taking different ways to the Jewel of Truth cannot hurt you. It is only the person who says "My way is the only way," whom you have to fear.

* * *

Please Draw a Tree

Part One

Since we've already been in a forest, I'd like you to draw a tree. What kind of tree? I don't care. Any kind. What kind of tree do you like? What kind of tree did you see in your forest? What kind of tree are you good at drawing?

Now don't make more of this than you need to. It really doesn't matter what kind of tree you draw and I really don't care how good of an artist you are. In fact, to be perfectly honest, it's not really about the tree.

A lot of what we'll be doing here is about sharing thoughts, feelings, and experiences. That's some pretty intimate and serious communication going on. So, before we go any further, I'd like to know if we can share a thought on the most basic level. When I ask you to draw a tree, am I asking clearly enough for you to understand that I really want you to draw a tree?

We've only got one shot at this. Am I communicating here? Am I getting through? That's all I want to know.

Yes? You know what I want? Super. So, draw a tree.

* * *

Part Two

Okay. What say we take a look at your tree. You didn't draw one?

(Psst. If you already drew your tree, skip this part and go straight to Part Three of this game. As for the vast majority of you, read on.)

Look. There's no reason to get hung up over it or start going around carrying fifty shades of guilt. Just be aware that what we're doing here is really interactive, and if you don't play the games and take an active part, you might finish the course, but you're not going to experience the payoff. You with me?

I mean, you wouldn't think twice about following directions, clicking on stuff, and even becoming some weird character just to play an online game. So why is it so tough to do the same thing here while you're listening to me talk inside your head?

Anyway, what's done is done, or not done as the case may be. I'm going into the kitchen to get another cup of coffee. Take advantage of the break and draw a tree. I'll see you shortly.

(Don't move on to Part Three until you draw the tree.)

* * *

Part Three

Okay. I'm back, and you've drawn a tree. Good. So, show me. How? I don't care. Paste it on your forehead and point it towards where these words are coming from. Tele-transport it to my desk. Create an imaginary being who can travel between dimensions and place it behind one of my frontal lobes. Use your imagination. Just get it over here, and let me have a second to look at it. Thanks.

...
   ...
...

(Sigh!) This is what I was afraid of. In fact, I pretty much figured this was going to happen. It almost always does.

Look. How difficult was it? I asked you to draw a tree, right? And did you draw a tree? I think not. Look again.

Half a tree. That's what you drew.

I didn't ask you to draw the top half of a tree, the part above the ground, or the part that's easy to see. I asked you to draw a tree. And you figured you understood, right?

So where are the roots? Aren't roots an integral part of a tree? Of course they are. You know that. Every tree has them. But did you draw roots on your tree? Nope. You see what I mean by communication being so hard?

But it's not your fault. You didn't draw roots on your tree because our society encourages us to focus only on what can be seen and measured. This is what the scientific bias of proof and measurement has done to our conception of reality. You're not the only one this has happened to.

(By the way, if you - the I reading these words right now - did draw roots on your tree, way to go! You are clearly in the minority.)

Either way, you have now entered the forest, adding new thoughts and experiences enroute. It's been said already but bears repeating: As you move ahead, don't accept what I say here without experiencing it for yourself. Trust in your own judgment, not what someone else tells you, not even the person writing these words. And don't be afraid to ask yourself how you know the things you already think you know. Keep your inner and outer I open. And especially, recognize that sudden knowing experience...

Trust it when it happens. Remember it as being real.

Also remember, there is no right way or wrong way for you to go, at least as long as you don't hurt others and get in their way. You get to do your own thing, create your own path, go where you want, and do what you want when you get there. And so do others. We all have our own talents, skills, and abilities. There are so many different people with so many different paths.

And with that in mind, let's move on.

* * *

How Do You Know What You Know?

Here's an interesting question: How do you know that you know something? I don't mean where did you find an answer to some specific question you had. I mean when you get an answer, how do you know you have the answer and don't keep looking to find it? In other words, what's the difference between thinking you have the answer, believing you have the answer, and knowing you have the answer? Simply put, how do you know that you know anything?

Until you can answer that question, you could find an answer you're looking for and never even know you knew it. Wouldn't that be a bummer?

The brilliant Zen philosopher and writer, Alan Watts, once penned a limerick about knowing. It goes like this:

> There was a young man who said though
> It seems that I know that I know,
> What I would like to see
> Is the I that sees me
> When I know that I know that I know.

The issue is not which parts of the brain perform the functions that create knowing. There are enough scientists working with rats, wires, and computer printouts to figure that out. The more interesting question is, "What does knowing feel like"? We don't need fancy equipment and a government grant to do this. We just need the ability to be aware of our inner awareness, something we've already begun doing.

Questions are a big giveaway to not knowing.

> Questions can be directed outwardly: *"Excuse me, sir, how do you get to Carnegie Hall?"*
>
> Questions can also be directed inwardly: *"Where did I put that phone number?"*

Of course, a lack of questions doesn't mean knowing exists. There's a lot in this world I don't want to know about, and I'm glad I don't. Or I may have gotten the wrong information and thought I knew something I didn't. In either scenario, I won't be asking questions, inside or outside.

Questions, of course, cause thinking, which is not to be confused with knowing. They are two separate and distinct experiences. Thinking is a "figuring out" process that proceeds mentally and sequentially, step by mental step. Thinking may indeed lead to knowing, but it is not the experience of knowing, itself.

How do we know? Well, think about it. When we finally get an answer to what we've been looking for and experience knowing, we switch our focus to the next thing we don't know and start asking questions about that.

>Outwardly: *"Did you say 'practice?"'*

>Inwardly: *"Now, why was I supposed to call?"*

Plus, there's an actual somatic difference between thinking and knowing. Thinking feels as if the process is taking place within our heads, while that feeling can vary based on what we happen to be thinking about. It can be relaxed and casual, intense and almost painful. We've all gotten headaches at some point in our lives from studying too hard or thinking too much.

Knowing, on the other hand, is a gut feeling located somewhere in our solar plexus. It feels the same no matter what subject we've been thinking about.

>Outwardly: *"Oh. It's a joke. I get it."*

>Inwardly: *"Ah, yes. I remember. I got it."*

You know - and you know you know. There is nothing to think about. With knowing, there is no question at all. That's what makes it knowing.

Of course, as fully functioning humans who are able to practice deception, we can pretend to know something when we don't. For example, if the teacher starts talking about a book you were supposed to have read and you nod your head as if you have, even though the teacher doesn't know you don't know, at least until the exam, you know you don't know. And that's what we're talking about after all, our own experience of knowing or not knowing.

Interesting, isn't it? Not knowing about a subject produces a definite feeling of knowing - knowing that you don't know! There is a surety in the feeling of knowing you don't know something that's the same as the feeling of knowing that you do know something. Take a minute. Don't just think about it — *feel* it. Fascinating.

It turns out knowing about knowing is not nearly as hard as talking about knowing. Plus, personal experience is so much better for learning than listening to someone else talk about their own experiences. So, check out this experiential game called, appropriately enough, the "Knowing Game".

Knowing Game

Respond to the following questions one at a time. Proceed as rapidly as you can; however, no guessing. Knowing is important. Knowing that you know - or not. Take time to play the game; otherwise, you will only be able to talk about knowing without really knowing it. Know what I mean?

Option One: If you know you know the answer, say "I know this answer," out loud, with conviction, but only if you *know* you know. Note what it feels like to know you know and where that feeling is located. Then go on to the next question.

Option Two: If you know you do not know the answer, say "I do not know this answer," out loud, with the same level of conviction, but only if you *know* you do not know. Note what it feels like to know you do not know and where that feeling is located. Then go on to the next question.

Option Three: If you are unsure about whether or not you know the answer to a given question, take a few minutes to think about it. Ask someone. Look in a book. Google it. Ask Siri or Alexa. Do what it takes to find the answer and note where that feeling of looking for the answer is located. After either finding the answer, or deciding you do not wish to spend any more time searching for it, say "I know this answer," or "I do not know this answer," whichever is the case, out loud and with conviction. Then go on to the next question.

Don't forget, you don't have to say the actual answers out loud. You only have to say whether you know the answer or not. Got it? Great. Here are the questions:

* * *

- How much is two plus two?

- What are the colors of the American flag?

- Who was the first human in space?

- What did you have for dinner two nights ago?

- How many squares are there on a chessboard?

- What is my wife's middle name?

- What does a zymometer measure?

* * *

Great. Nice job. Now let's head to the Post Game Wrap-up.

* * *

Post Game Wrap-up

Okay. Having played the game (you did, right?), you should now be able to talk about knowing from within the experience of knowing itself.

For those questions you clearly know, such as "How much is two and two?" You simply said, "I know this answer." It was easy. You may not have even thought of the actual answer at all. You just know you know it. And you should have had an equally strong response for the colors of the flag as you did for two plus two. You said, "I know this answer." You didn't even think about it. Piece of cake.

That feeling of knowing without question or doubt was located deep inside your gut, which is why it is called a gut feeling. Duh! That feeling was the same even though the questions and the answers were different.

Now, when you knew you did not know the answer to the question, "What is my wife's middle name"? it was just as easy and immediate to say, "I do not know this answer." How could you possibly know it? You've never met her and she never uses it.

That, too, should have been a gut feeling since there was no thinking and the brain was not involved. There was no questioning here, no trying to find an answer. And even though one response has content, while the other does not, the feeling of knowing you know or knowing you don't know is a similar sure gut reaction of certainty in both cases.

Knowing is absolute. With knowing there is no question. In fact, this is what makes it knowing. Anything less would be believing, theorizing, supposing, guessing, or hoping or any number of less than total gut feeling experiences. There is nothing wrong with these experiences, but they are not absolute, visceral, gut feel knowing. Are you with me?

Now the feeling was quite different when you were unsure about whether or not you knew the answer and had to think about it. Whether it was something you could find via some external source, the first man in space, or something you could only answer by searching your own memory, like your dinner menu, that's when mind came into play. What you did next, the steps leading up to knowing such as thinking, reading, going online, asking others, and so forth, that process was head stuff, whether you got an answer or not.

There are times we just give up. We search inside and outside looking for answers we never find without ever experiencing the feeling of satisfaction we get from knowing. And that's one way we know that knowing is clearly separate from thinking, the process leading up to it, even if the final knowing is that I don't know.

So, having played the "Knowing Game", you should now be able to say with complete conviction that you know several facts about knowing that you may not have known before. Not just because you read them somewhere but because you experienced them personally. Namely, you know that:

1) Thinking takes place in the head while knowing takes place in the gut;

2) The feeling of knowing is the same regardless of the content of knowing;

3) Knowing you do not know is a feeling of knowing.

It is good to remember that you know these things as we move ahead and attempt to examine our own consciousness. It will save you from having to repeat steps in the process because you doubt what you now know you know.

By the way, just in case you had not experienced the full flush of knowing the above questions, aside from your dinner, which only you and the person you might have eaten dinner with can know (or not), the answers are:

- four
- red-white-and-blue
- Yuri Gagarin
- 64
- Mae
- degree of fermentation

There, now you know!

> *Yup!*

You sure?

> *Yup, now I know.*

Good.

* * *

(Psst, those answers I just gave you. Are you sure they're the right answers?)

> *Huh? Whaddya mean?*

Check this out. Unless you already knew all the answers, including my wife's middle name, you would have no way of knowing whether the answers I just gave you were the correct ones or not. And now that you know that the answers I just gave you might not be true, the confidence of knowing what you felt in your gut just a moment ago should be history. Interesting.

Not only that, if I had not warned you just now that the answers might be false, such a thought would have never crossed your mind. Admit it. You *know* that it's true.

Without that warning, you would now think you knew the answers and conceivably would have told them to a friend as truth adding, "Oh, I read it somewhere." See how easily misinformed or unscrupulous people can manipulate and take advantage of us?

This is the very kind of "knowing" that Descartes' rules of reason declare to be invalid. It is also why absolute "knowing" must remain an individual process and why we must experience for ourselves - from the inside - everything we want to say we know for certain.*

Aren't consciousness games fun?

Congratulations. You've made it through the preliminaries and background preparation needed to experience New Consciousness. Not everyone gets this far. Many give up when they have to go inside and examine themselves and their preconceived ideas. You did it and are none the worse for wear. As we move

---

* Actually, the answers I gave you are true. But I wouldn't be surprised if you wanted to look them up somewhere else just to be sure.

forward, try to remember what you have experienced up to this point. Stay open to your feelings and own what you know you know.

Using the forest analogy, we've slogged through the underbrush and bushes around the periphery, carrying the equipment to set up base camp. That being accomplished, we can now head deeper into the tall trees surrounding the Jewel of Truth, deeper into the forest where the first real taste of the evolutionary New Consciousness experience will occur. As we move on, please direct your attention to the center of the screen in the center of your mind.

✶ ✶ ✶

It is by non-attachment that we grow...

By letting go of preconceived notions...

Ideas that have outlived their usefulness...

It's time to learn something new.

✶ ✶ ✶

Seeing the Light

Part One

You are a highly trained, scientifically and technically aware, international operative representing government and commercial interests on the leading edge of the study of consciousness and the human mind. Your assignment: Find out how consciousness works.

Tracking down a hot lead late one night in the laboratory of a competitor, you are attacked from behind, and knocked unconscious.

You come to awareness lying on your back in complete darkness with no idea of where you are or how you got there. Luckily, everything seems to be in good working order as you flex, shake off the mental cobwebs, and try to figure out what to do next.

Suddenly, a powerful and brilliant light from above floods the absolute blackness, and you find yourself momentarily blinded by the contrast. You reflexively close your eyes and turn away, but the light has made it possible for you to see. As your eyes begin to adjust, you note that you are on the floor inside a large dome-shaped building, now illuminated by a single source of light high above your head and much too strong to look at directly. Fascinating how the light is illuminating everything in the building except itself.

Unable to look directly at the light because of its brightness, with no further information than what your sensory experience has already given you, you realize that as long as you are there on the floor, there is no way you can answer any questions about the light with any degree of certainty, such as how it works, why it works, and who, if anyone, is in charge. Without further facts, whatever you have come up with is merely speculation, and your academic training and scientific rigor will not permit you to make unsupported claims. Let's face it. There is nothing about the light you know for sure.

The only thing you can know for sure is what you experienced personally and firsthand. It had been dark. Now it is light. The light had been off. Now it is on. Whatever else you may not know, that much you know, right?

(Answer before moving on)

* * *

Part Two

Psst! Did you actually answer the question from Part One before reading this?

Now, I'm not just talking about thinking about it. What I'm asking is, did you stop looking at the words in front of your eyes, visualize yourself on the floor of something that looks like the Astrodome, experience the feeling of going from darkness to light, and actually answer the question?

You did? Great! Hold on as I talk to the vast majority of you reading this right now.

Yo, guys. Didn't I talk to you back at the tree? Get with it. This isn't even as complicated as drawing a tree. You simply have to experience what is happening and know this stuff for yourself, not because I tell you it is so, right? Let's try again.

So, given the scenario we just set up, this is what you experienced personally and firsthand...

"It had been dark. Now it is light. The light had been off. Now it is on. Whatever else you may not know, that much you know, right?"

(Answer before moving on)

* * *

Part Three

It had been dark...

                                                          ...yes

Now it is light...

                                                          ...yes

The light had been off...

                                                          ...yes

Now the light is on...

                                                          ...yes

Agreed?

                                                          ...yes

* * *

Well, not necessarily.

                                                    ...really?

Get this. You can certainly say, as a result of your direct knowing, that you had experienced darkness and now are experiencing light. And with the Western penchant for putting names on processes and turning verbs into nouns, you could even say, "it" had been dark, and now, "it" is light. Whatever "it" is.

However, you cannot say with absolute confidence that what you experienced occurred because a light, which had been off, is now on. Although that would be a reasonable explanation, especially since the invention of the light bulb, it is pure supposition, since at least one other scenario could produce the same experiential result.

Take a moment. Can you see it?

* * *

What if a lens-shaped aperture, similar to a camera shutter, had suddenly opened in the ceiling, revealing a brilliant and powerful light source that was already on and located just above the roof on the outside of the building? The opening of the shutter would have flooded the inside of the building with light from this already illuminated source.

Lying there on the floor below, your experience would be the same as if a light inside the building had gone on, right? A sudden change from darkness to light. And because you are unable to look at and see the details and know the workings of the light-producing mechanism because of its brightness, there would be no possible way for you to tell which of the two processes had actually taken place and changed your world. Did a light come on? Did a lens open up? From where you are there is no way to know. Interesting.

What is more interesting, however, and the critical issue at this point is not even which mode of illumination is lighting up your otherwise dark surroundings. This doesn't matter. What does matter is the realization that once it is clear that there are two equally valid and equally logical possibilities that yield the exact same sensory experience, *it becomes impossible for the rational and logical mind, your scientific mind, to hold onto any one explanation as being the only possible one.*

* * *

Part Four

Okay. Let's apply our experience with the light to the issue of consciousness.

Cognitive science and other physical disciplines have clearly established the relationship between mind and brain. The more evolved the brain, the more evolved the mind. Our brains are developed beyond those of dogs, which in turn are developed beyond those of frogs, which are developed beyond those of slugs, and so on. This is an observable fact.

As expected, the perceptual and cognitive capacities and capabilities of the mind at each different level map a clear, direct relationship with the development of the brain. We're all in agreement.

However, what has been presumed to be a logical conclusion within the scientific community regarding an underlying causal relationship between brain and mind, that as the brain grows and develops it creates the attributes of consciousness we call mind, turns out to be pure supposition.

As with the appearance of light in the thought experiment we have just done, there is another completely different explanation of the brain/mind relationship. It is just as valid and just as possible as the causal explanation of modern science, though it leads to completely different conclusions about the nature of reality and consciousness, itself.

What if the brain, through its measurable development and evolution, rather than creating an internal light of consciousness out of dark nothingness, was actually opening us up to an awareness of a light of consciousness that already exists external to us?

Is it possible? Why not?

Why not, indeed! Back when we were inside the building, experiencing the light, we couldn't tell whether it was coming from a light source under the roof or whether there was a hole in the roof revealing a light source above the roof. In an exact parallel from within our body, looking at the source of our own consciousness, we have absolutely no way of knowing whether it is self-contained within us or flooding us through an aperture from an external source. Think about it. From within, there is no possible way we can tell the difference. Once it's in our heads it's too late to tell where it came from.

Remember, all the neuroscientific studies ever done to demonstrate the relationship between brain and mind are still valid. The observable features still hold. The more evolved the brain, the greater the capacity of the mind. Only now, the brain is viewed not as a mechanism whose development, like the operating of a rheostat, turns on a light and makes it ever brighter. The brain now becomes a mechanism whose development, like the operating of a camera shutter, widens and allows ever greater access to an already existing brightness.

What is more interesting, however, and the critical issue at this point is not even which mode of illumination is lighting up your otherwise dark surroundings. This doesn't matter. What does matter is the realization that once it is clear that there are two equally valid and equally logical possibilities that yield the exact same sensory experience, *it becomes impossible for the rational and logical mind, your scientific mind, to hold onto any one explanation as being the only possible one.*

* * *

Post Game Wrap Up

Amazing, isn't it? There are two equally possible explanations for where our consciousness comes from, yet only one has dominated scientific thinking for the past several hundred years. It seems so obvious. Both should be considered.

And yet, if accepted, it would require a major paradigm shift that would reshape all of Western thought. Is such a shift even possible? Well, of course it is. That's how progress happens. That's how we have evolved to where we are now, and that is how we will continue to evolve into a New Consciousness.

There used to be a time when everyone was certain that Earth was flat. Then brave adventurers started sailing home from places where they should have fallen off. Talk about screwing with the belief system.

It was less than 500 years ago when we were equally as sure that the Sun went around Earth and we were in the center of things. You just had to look up and see it was true with your own eyes, for gosh sakes. But, after Copernicus, with one small change in consciousness so that we now could see the Sun holding steady while Earth rotates around it, humanity's entire understanding shifts, making it possible to comprehend an even greater reality.

I wonder how long it took for the average enquiring mind of the time to actually accept that Earth orbited the Sun instead of the other way around. You can just see the headlines in the supermarket tabloids back in 1543:

POLISH ASTRONOMER SAYS EARTH SPINS LIKE A TOP!

Interesting how the eye of mainstream science, while freeing us from the distorting lens of a parochial medieval theology, has nonetheless colored our subconscious reality in the exact same way with a distorting lens of its own. Everything must be measurable, or else it is not real! Just as those trapped in the theological mindset could not conceive of any other way of viewing reality than the will of an almighty God, so it is with those of the purely scientific mindset who cannot recognize that their view is just as skewed.

Think about it. Question it. Feel it. Examine it. You can't help but know, based on your personal experience, that it is impossible to tell for certain whether your consciousness, your awareness of being, the feeling of I at your very core, is being generated from within your brain or being received by your brain through an "opening" from outside. *Remember, once it's in your head, it's too late to find out where it came from.*

As logical, thinking, rational people, we have to accept this as a possibility. After all, anything less than considering all possibilities would be unscientific, right?

Let's look at consciousness from this other perspective, which posits that the conscious experience, that very feeling of I AM that we all have at our deepest core, is not created by the brain but received by the brain from an ultimate reality that fills the entire Universe. Call it what you will: God, the Singularity, the source of The Big Bang, whatever you want. According to New Consciousness, this universal I AM is the underlying root of everything.

This would mean that all of what we call void, space, emptiness, nothingness, the vast reaches of the known and the unknown, is actually filled with an immeasurable, non-physical, all-pervading, undifferentiated consciousness.

Could it be? Why not? It fits with both religion and quantum physics. Plus, from inside of consciousness, how could we possibly know? It's like the old Sufi saying, "I don't know who first discovered water, but I'm sure it wasn't a fish."

Let's stop momentarily and see if we can put this different but reasonable way of explaining consciousness into simple rules. I call it the New Consciousness Paradigm. But a name, as you know by now, is unimportant.

* * *

The New Consciousness Paradigm

First premise: *Consciousness exists in everything, whether we know it's there or not.*

Consciousness exists out there, and also in here. It is inside and outside each and every atom of everything that exists in whatever size universe we can imagine. And if we can theoretically visualize a reality between inside and outside, it would fill that space, too.

We exist in consciousness, and consciousness exists in us in much the same way that water exists in a living sponge and the living sponge exists in water. And like the water in relationship to the sponge, consciousness doesn't care whether we know it is there or not.

Although consciousness is the building block of everything that exists, everything is not aware of being conscious. Consciousness exists independent of its being known, independent of our awareness of it, and independent of our ability to measure it. Consciousness just is.

Second premise: *A being's material nature affects how consciousness is experienced.*

The relationship between consciousness and material things is similar to how radio waves, passing unnoticed through space, are only turned into sound by machines designed to receive them and tuned to their particular frequency. Consciousness has many different frequencies and is infinitely more complicated than radio waves.

We know that the radio does not produce the music that plays through its speakers. It is receiving and playing sounds that already exist. Just as with radios and sound waves, the receiver's capability determines how much, what frequencies, and with what clarity total consciousness is received and rebroadcast.

Total consciousness flows through rocks, plants, and animals just as easily and completely as it flows through humans. Humans just have more ways available for interacting with consciousness. The amount of consciousness a thing picks up, processes, and displays also determines how evolved humans think it is. We think we're at the top of the ladder, but that's another story.

Third premise: *Consciousness is experienced as I AM.*

I, the reader of this sentence, am a conscious being and experience I AM. Therefore, a new thought has now entered my mind.

Yes, my friend, according to New Consciousness, just like all beings, you are an actual manifestation of the Universal Oneness.

Feel the enormity of it all and enjoy the feeling. Recognize you are not just some small, insignificant creature crawling around on this planet by chance but are a part of Universal Creation itself. Look at your particular likes, dislikes, skills, and talents, recognize their uniqueness, and ask how you can use them to improve life, not just for yourself but for all life.

By living in the awareness of New Consciousness you can help keep humanity from destroying itself as, together, we create a world of perpetual peace and universal understanding. Yes, my friend. We can do this.

You are. I am. And, we are One. Welcome to the experience of New Consciousness.

Part Two:

Living the Oneness Within

* * *

Spirit spanning cognition.
Intellectual activity in the light of spiritual awareness.
Really very simple.
Above all a knowing.
        not a belief...
        not a guessing...
        not a hoping...
        not a wanting...
But a knowing.

One single overriding consciousness
        pervading the universe...
        ...everything and every process.

One single overriding consciousness
        manifesting the physical world...
        ...in an unbelievably diverse number of ways,

One of which is you... the one now having thoughts about
        ... a single overriding consciousness.

Where Do I Go From Here?

Congratulations! By completing Part One of the Handbook you have overcome the most significant hurdle there is to experiencing New Consciousness. You have opened your mind to the possibility that the consciousness that defines your very feeling of existing wasn't simply created by your brain, but actually received by your brain from a larger universal source.

Even though you know that each of us is absolutely unique, you now know that from the perspective of New Consciousness, the I AM experience, we all feel at our absolute core is the very Oneness that created the entire universe and everything that exists within it. How incredible is that! My I AM and your I AM are the same I AM. That's New Consciousness. And since you are now aware that it is just as valid a possibility as the old way of looking at consciousness, it's time to use that knowledge and see what evolutionary experiences it gives you.

We're going to start taking incredible journeys, moving your mind into places you never thought it could go. Think about it for a moment. Since you are now open to the possibility that your consciousness doesn't actually exist 'inside' you, but only feels like it does, you can let go and ride that consciousness to any place you want to take it throughout the universe. Is that cool or what? But we're getting ahead of ourselves and it does take practice. So, we're going to firm up that knowledge first so it doesn't slip away when you're not paying attention.

As you have already discovered, this knowledge is neither technical, complex, nor difficult to understand. Nor is it based on any religious or spiritual beliefs, though it validates and agrees with many major world religions, not to mention the findings of modern quantum physics. New Consciousness is simply a logical evolutionary awareness available to anyone who wishes to find and use it, requiring no great training, study, or advanced degrees to access and apply in life.

All that is necessary for experiencing New Consciousness, as you have already seen, is an open mind, a scientific mind, a willingness to explore that mind, and the strength of will to affirm what you experience in that exploration, even if it goes against the naysayers who fear any change in the status quo. As a result, you will be able to enter a different dimension where you experience the ends of the universe in time and space and understand the purpose of life, both on the grandest cosmic and the most intimately personal scales. This is what you are about to discover.

Only you, of course, know why you find the subject of New Consciousness of interest. Maybe you have had psychic visions, dreams and out-of-body experiences you're finding it hard to wrap your mind around. Maybe you want to find a way of explaining them that doesn't make you feel like some sort of weirdo. If so, New Consciousness can provide the answer.

I once had a friend, since deceased, who as a little girl used to be able to tell who was calling when the phone rang or who had sent the letters that were sitting out in the mailbox. "Stop doing that," she recalled her mother yelling at her, "Father Anthony thinks we're strange enough already." She was not strange, of course. She was just ahead of her time.

Maybe you're interested in New Consciousness because you look at the rampant chaos and confusion in the world around you and think this can't be all there is. Well, it's not. It's simply where we are at the moment. Apply New Consciousness to your thinking and you will soon be looking at a different world from a larger perspective, while recognizing that patterns exist and things aren't quite as scattered and random as they look. This can be kind of comforting even if we can't see the absolute way it's all going to turn out.

Or perhaps you're interested in New Consciousness because you really do want to shift your personal paradigm and help humanity evolve into a better place. You see the evolutionary writing on the wall and want to be in the forefront of what-comes-next as far as human consciousness goes. Fantastic. That's the reason the Handbook was written. When enough of us do see, feel, and live the connection between us, it will absolutely change the future of life on Earth.

* * *

New Consciousness Defined

"How can you define consciousness?" asked a noted professor at a symposium I once attended on the subject. "You can't," he answered himself, "it's too subjective."

Yet, based on what we have experienced, you and I must disagree with him. Yes, our individual worldly interactions are absolutely unique for each one of us because of the particular filters that make us who we are. But as we enter deep within ourselves, past the point where social, physical, mental, emotional, and spiritual differences matter in the experiment, we approach a shared common experience. An experience so common and universal, in fact, that it can no longer be considered subjective.

At our very core we each share the conscious experience of just plain 'being'. This feeling of personal consciousness is exactly the same for every single one of us even though the unique characteristics surrounding each individual's consciousness are different. This means that consciousness, itself, is universal and objective. And that's where the professor went wrong. He didn't go far enough inside.

New Consciousness is knowing that when we say I AM we are speaking fact and that anything we say after that to describe ourselves: male, female, black, white, yellow, red, rich, poor, Hindu, Christian, Muslim, Jew, Buddhist, and so on are just filters and adjectives through which we view and experience the world.

Up until now, humans have related to the adjectives that separate us: the bodies, ideas, experiences, emotions, everything that makes us look and feel different and separate from each other - me from you - you from me. We find fault simply because others have different adjectives from us and do things differently than we do. And because of that, we act towards each other in ways that are less than humane, to put it mildly.

Yet deep inside us, deep inside those different adjectives that separate us, is something we all have in common: the feeling that I AM. And that's true for everyone, every single seemingly separate one of us.

When we look out and see that we are physically separate from each other, naturally we think each feeling of I AM is separate from each other's feeling of I AM as well. That makes sense when you're looking out with your eyes. However, I AM doesn't just *feel* the same for each of us, it *is the same* for all of us. Deep down inside where we all feel our I, we are all connected. My I is not just the same *as* your I - it *is* the same I. Pure consciousness is I AM.

Call I AM the God of religion, call it the Dark Energy of quantum physics, call it the Singularity. Call it whatever you want! It doesn't matter what you call it. That's what is at our core. Inside the adjectives. Inside the filters.

Inside the differences. Pure Consciousness. That's what we share. Our I. Having come this far, you don't just believe it, you know it!

While we are surrounded by the stuff that defines each of us as individuals and makes us different from others, it is the same I AM that is in the center of us all.

The goal is not to think we are the impulses and urges, thoughts and emotions, talents and handicaps that make us unique, but to look at these impulses and urges, thoughts and emotions, talents and handicaps from within them and say, "What is the best I can do with this stuff for the good of all?"

(Psst! I know it appears that we are repeating some concepts you already read in Part One. Well, you're right. However, reading that we are all connected by the Oneness within us is one thing. Knowing it is another. Living it is yet another. Reinforcing the idea of New Consciousness to make it feel comfortable and natural will ultimately help you make this evolutionary leap and that, after all, is what the Handbook is all about.)

* * *

Inside - Outside

As life has evolved on Earth, producing ever more complex housing for consciousness, a level has been reached where the human conscious experience exists as an experiential synapse between inside and outside.

"Synapse", according to a well-worn American College Dictionary in my possession, is defined as "the region of contact between processes of two or more nerve cells, across which an impulse passes." Which is to say, a synapse represents those places along our nervous system where there's no continuous physical path for an impulse to get from one side to the other; where a leap of some sort is required. We're going to discover that synapse is a good word to use for the human I experience.

Let's start with the fact that in the normal human process of living, our focus of attention is constantly moving back and forth between the world outside and the world inside. Most times we have absolutely no idea where we are.

In the dream state, clearly, this is true. I can live rip-roaring adventures and heart-rending dramas in dreams, thinking I'm acting and interacting with the world outside while I'm actually functioning only in the inner reality of my mind, while my body is lying there in external reality as an inert lump. In the dream, I'm not even aware that there is an external lump lying there, except in lucid dreaming, but that's another experience we don't need to get into here.

However, dreams are not the only place this happens. Often, in the midst of daily waking life, I put my body on autopilot and let my thoughts slip into some inner channel, some hypnotic trail of reason and logic, or intuition and spirit, or some mystic combination of the two. Such trips take attention from the physical reality of the here and now, what I am actually perceiving with my senses, and lead to an inner place that is separated by a wall of consciousness from those senses.

This non-conscious shift into an inner world experience can occur while driving up a long straight highway, walking along the beach at sunset, or sitting in a class listening to a boring lecture. We've all experienced that suddenness of being jarred back into our bodies when the car ahead swerves out of their lane, or we realize how cold it's gotten, or the professor calls our name. We were "somewhere else," and now we are back. And we didn't even know we were gone.

The senses, of course, being necessary for physical survival, still take in information, non-consciously, as a safety device for the body, even if we are not paying attention. Should parameters exceed some preprogrammed load factor, the information is brought to the awareness of the occupant. Which is to say, we become conscious of that particular sensory input: the swerving car, the chill on the skin, the sound of our name. This non-conscious self-monitoring is what allows cognitive beings, such as humans, to go on autopilot and experience inner reality in the first place.

The other end of the spectrum is represented by moments of complete lucidity and total awareness of the physical world generated by peak experiences of sight, sound, feeling, smell or taste that bring our focus 100% to the sensory data being received. Most often, this is brought on by inputs signaling danger, such as a warning cry or the smell of smoke. However, it can also be derived from pleasurable phenomena, through taste and smell, for example, or through orgasm.

In such a state, there is no inner reflection, thought, reasoning, or mystical musing. Consciousness is totally focused on the incoming sensory data. This isn't to say that we are conscious of all incoming data. Rather, it's that we are only aware of external inputs, even though we may be missing much of the totality of what our senses are actually receiving. The truth is, at any given point, we actually only monitor one sensory input at a time. The process is similar to the way we think we are reading the whole dashboard of the car as we drive, when in reality we can only actually monitor and register one dial at a time.

Persons who are only focused internally, as in the case of coma or severe mental disturbance, are unable to relate to the outer world at all and cannot take care of themselves and their basic survival needs. We must, at the very least, be able to relate externally to the food placed in front of our mouth in order to react to that outer reality and eat. Even the most ascetic Indian yogis know that at least a minimum level of external awareness is necessary to live and survive in the world.

At the other extreme, people who display only external focus would have no awareness of Self or I consciousness and would act only instinctively. They either wouldn't have individual thoughts, or wouldn't be aware of such thoughts if they appeared, which experientially amounts to the same thing. While this level of consciousness may work for ants, fish and termites, it's certainly not a human characteristic, as we currently define human.

The bottom line, clearly, is that if we remain in either inside or outside exclusively, we are not functioning as a normal, operating, self-sufficient human being. In order to do so, we must go back and forth between the two realities.

Although this polarity between inside and outside is not difficult to think about or talk about, true awareness of inside and outside, just like everything else, ultimately requires an embodiment based on personal experience. The concept is similar to thinking you know, and knowing you know, a difference you've already experienced.

To understand and experience this synapse, we first have to make sure we truly know and experience the difference between Inside and Outside, a concept you undoubtedly learned before graduating kindergarten. Well, at least you think you learned it.

Simply being aware, for example, that an empty box on the floor has an inside and an outside does not qualify as knowing the difference. That requires nothing more than a vague remembering of an authority figure that appeared at some time in your life, a parent or a teacher most likely, relating two particular parts of an external object to their human constructed names.

Teacher: "*This part of the box is called the inside;*
this part of the box is called the outside."

Even knowing how to use the box doesn't convey the experience of inside and outside. Although it goes beyond the purely definitional by requiring an understanding of certain simple laws of physics, both aspects of the box are still, experientially speaking, out there.

You: "*Put the ball there, inside, it stays;*
put the ball there, outside; it rolls away."

Only by placing yourself in the role of the box, as the actual boundary between inside and outside, can you truly experience the polar reality of each.

Box: "*Facing one direction is inside me;*
facing the other direction is outside me."

At least that's what the box would experience if it had awareness of the I consciousness flowing through it like we do. For that's all a box is, after all, an experiential separator of inside and outside. Unfold it, and it's no longer even a box, but merely hard-to-dispose of garbage.

For most of us, the edge of the body is the dividing line between inside and outside, the boundary that defines our sense of where I stop and you begin. Logically speaking, there are many good and valid reasons for accepting this obvious body-boundary definition. For one, the physical self is the one I am most familiar and comfortable with, the one that defines whom I feed, bathe, clothe, and recognize in the mirror. And it's what keeps other people from standing where I am standing while I am standing there.

The body boundary also defines the one who can touch my underarm without it tickling, is the basis for designing movie and airline seats, voter registration, and for taking numbers in a bakery. It is the definition the criminal and judicial system uses to place blame and mete out punishment for infractions against society, except in judgments of insanity, where the person and the person's body are judged to be in two separate places at the time of the crime. It's also the one the IRS uses for filing taxes, except for joint and corporate returns, where the physical body is considered only part of a larger legal body.

Yet despite some compelling arguments in its favor, it's not an absolute given that the edge of the body is the definitive dividing line between:

I ... me ... inside ... in here ... on one side

... and ...

You ... it ... outside ... out there ... on the other

In fact, anthropologically speaking, for most of human development, identification of the individual self with a tribe or clan rather than an individual body was the rule rather than the exception. It's still the norm in many indigenous societies and was the common reality for emerging Indo-European culture as recently as the Greek city-states of only several thousand years ago. Even in our modern-day culture of staunch individualism, as a result of idol worship, nationalism, and religious fanaticism, to name a few, it's not unusual for individuals to equate their I with power or possessions, a cause or ideal, a group or a family, or even a sports team.

This important question of where to place the boundary between I and "apparent not-I" will appear later in the Handbook. For now, we need merely recognize that no matter where we put the boundary, its very existence indicates that inside and outside, the differences between you and me, are experienced as pointing in polar complimentary or opposite directions.

It is here that we share the common phenomenological experience of I as seen through different eyes. Though the content of our lives will be different, the feeling of Self, what we mean when we say I, and the recognition of something that is not-I is the same for all and exists at our very core. It is the common shared human experience.

Now although the inner and outer worlds are both real, they present two very valid experiences with separate and distinct attributes that are polar complementary to each other. Though both are necessary for the human experience, it is their very natures that cause the problems with traditional scientific acceptance of an obvious reality.

Outer reality can be measured but provides no meaning.

Inner reality provides meaning but cannot be measured.

Another way of saying this, comprehensive and compatible with New Consciousness, as you shall soon see, is that the provable physical outside world is non-intuitive, while the intuitive spiritual inside world is non-provable. Mull this over for a while. I think you'll find that the human I, capable of accessing both inner and outer reality as the ultimate unifying experience, exists somewhere in between the two, bridging the gap between meaning and measurement, much like that synapse we've already discussed.

* * *

* * *

New Consciousness...   *...Old Consciousness*
opening the shutter...   *...a light going on*
onto an existing light...   *...in the darkness*
I AM   *I AM*
I   *I*

here's the fun part...   *...once it's in your head*
you're free to be...   *...it's too late*
whichever one...   *...to figure out*
you want to be...   *...how you got it*

...which is why...
...this evolutionary step...
is
voluntary

* * *

Looking Out/Looking In Game

The living body is constantly moving in and out, in and out, in a natural rhythm of breathing. The process is necessary to our very existence. Although breathing is usually an unconscious act that we do without thinking, it is possible to focus on our breathing and override its involuntary nature to some degree. This can be useful when we're underwater, in a smoke-filled room, or next to a 'bad dog,' to name a few.

The human mind also moves in and out on a regular and rhythmic basis. It, too, is a natural, unconscious aspect of who we are and just as critical to our 'being human'. With practice, we can have the same type of control over our mind as we do over our breathing. This awareness is important to what comes next.

* * *

Level One

Sit quietly. Become aware of the outer reality around you. Pick something out there that isn't I, something you could call, for want of a better name, Not-I.

(Examples: a tree, a water bottle, the sound of traffic, the smell of a rose, a photo of your favorite movie star. The possibilities are endless.)

Focus on it. What is it that makes you call this object it and not me? Are you sure?

Note that you see, hear, feel, smell, or taste it, but only after some aspect of it reaches your senses from *out there,* where it is. Your senses are connected with your body. They are part of your personal I experience. The input coming in through the senses is not. Can you tell the difference? Are you sure?

(A number of years ago, the grocery store on the corner half a block from where I lived used to bake the most magnificent scones every morning. You could not walk past without getting a whiff of absolute deliciousness that would make you think about scones. That smell was clearly coming from outside.)

Play with the inputs coming in to you. See things, hear sounds, smell odors, feel textures, taste flavors. Recognize that without these attributes coming through your senses, you would not be aware of anything outside of you. Become comfortable with your portals to the outside. Get familiar with where you are focusing your attention. Pay attention to where you are paying attention. Is it inside? or outside?

Tips for Optimum Play

Repetition at fixed times during the day and at the same location helps to solidify the experience.

Practicing at different locations and times of day helps to broaden the experience. When the awareness starts to come naturally, let it happen.

Look for patterns that might emerge, different feelings in similar places, similar thoughts with different people. Play with awareness. Have fun.

* * *

Level Two

Repeat Level One until you find a thought going through your mind that did not come from the outer reality around you, through your senses from the tree, the water bottle, the sound of traffic, the smell of the rose, or the photo of that movie star.

(Examples: remembering a conversation you had with a friend, wondering what's for dinner, giving a name or attribute to what you are focusing on such as pretty, red, or ditsy, congratulating yourself on not thinking an inner thought. The possibilities are endless.)

When you recognize an internal focus, refocus on the external again, and again, and again.

The time it takes for an internally focused thought to occur will vary. Eventually, however, such a thought crosses all minds; have no fear. It's the nature of being human, just like breathing.

(Sometimes, those years back, when I was sitting at my desk, I'd think about scones. But I couldn't smell the scones from my apartment. Clearly, that thought was coming from inside, just like it is now, when I am writing this and wishing they hadn't sold the store to people who don't bake scones.)

Do not berate yourself for having an unbidden internal thought. Just go back and focus externally again and again until you can see yourself operating within this very natural process of going back and forth between external focus and internal focus. Become familiar with what it feels like to focus inside and to focus outside.

Tips for Optimum Play

Try to trace your inner thoughts to some prior outer reality that may have triggered the idea. Was it something on the TV news, an incident that happened at work, a breakfast date with a friend?

Try to trace your outer reality to some prior inner reality, some personal taste or preference that is reflected in your physical setting. Play with awareness. Have fun.

* * *

Level Three

Once you know what internal focus and external focus each feel like, try to put this knowledge into practice in your daily life. Be truly aware of where your I is at all times.

(Examples: are you really watching the road while driving and talking on a cell phone? Are you really paying attention to your conversation while driving and talking on a cell phone? Can you really do both at the same time?)

Try to keep both inside and outside in mind at the same time. This is not easy. It's challenging. In fact, it's actually impossible. You can go back and forth really fast. So fast that it seems as if you're focusing both ways at once, but it's an illusion. It's the same as watching a movie that appears to show motion even though it's actually a series of still shots projected one right after the other.

Remember that 'keeping them both in mind' is an inside focus requiring a constant outside refocusing again in order to keep them both in mind.

This is where infinite spirals start, where you begin to see your awareness of your awareness of your awareness of your awareness, similar to looking into mirrors in a barber shop and seeing yourself receding off in infinite regression.

This ability to watch ourselves watch ourselves watch ourselves is part of the New Consciousness, a key to becoming the I that sees me.

Tips for Optimum Play

Get into a rhythm of watching yourself move back and forth between inside and outside. What does it feel like? Where is the I located who is watching this happen?

Is it getting easier to do? Compare 'now' with previous 'nows'. In what direction is the continuum of change occurring? Play with awareness. Have fun.

* * *

It's All About Balance

Let's take a break for a moment and stop to acknowledge just how far you have come since first deciding to look at reality from the perspective of New Consciousness. For starters, you are aware that your sense of Self, your very experience of existing, represents a synapse, a connection between the inner and outer worlds. On one side of the synapse, the inside, is the pure Absolute consciousness that exists within all. We may not be able to define it, but we can certainly *feel* it. It is the very feeling of existing, of being, of knowing that I AM. This is true for each and every one of us.

On the other side, the outside, is everything else. Everything else! This is the physical, emotional, and mental world of mind and body. It's the world you live in, the people you love, the things you know, the things you do, your thoughts and emotions, your actions and your dreams. Whereas pure absolute consciousness, your inner feeling of being is exactly the same as everyone else, your outer world, what your consciousness experiences, is completely different from everyone else. We are indeed snowflakes.

Not only that, but the world inside is constant. The Absolute never changes. You may not know much about it other than knowing I AM exists, but what other information do you really need?

Since the Absolute is who you really are on the inside, you can put that awareness on auto-pilot and focus attention in the other direction - *out there*. That is where things are constantly changing, where stuff happens that affects your life, where your actions affect the lives of others, and where you never know what to expect.

You could think of it this way: I am a gyroscope balanced on a string that has a fixed point on one end and a constantly moving point on the other end. If the moving end dips below the level of the fixed end, the gyroscope slides one way. If the moving end rises above the fixed end, the gyroscope slides the other way. Movement in both directions can occur even though only one end of the string is moving. My goal is to remain balanced between the two.

I go back and forth, balancing my consciousness between the polar complementaries of the fixed universal I AM inside and my moving personal life experiences outside. I exist at the boundary where the separate analogue tapes of each become a single double-sided digital experience. This is where inner and outer combine, where knowing and not knowing appear. Thus, the determinant of the synapse, the balancing point for my I at any given 'now' is based on where and how I define myself.

Knowing that I am connected in my inner reality to everything that exists through a common I lets me reframe my I and to view what was previously considered as "other" as "apparent not-self".* Nothing has changed in my outer reality because of the change in my point of view. Whatever was *out there* is still there and measurable. Only the inner understanding of who I am changes, along with the meaning given to whatever is observed.

In New Consciousness I still see each individual as a separate and distinct physical being. However, I also see them as separate aspects of a common I AM. Me, in another body, so to speak. Such a change of perspective has to affect how we all look at and treat other beings. At least it should. One never knows with humans.

In a parallel that quantum physics records in the material world as electrons jumping back and forth between one atomic orbit or another, I can now jump back and forth between levels of awareness at will. Depending on where I place my attention, I can experience different platforms for perception that alter my view of reality. Is what I am experiencing happening inside me or outside me? That depends on where I put my I.

Being in tune with all aspects of these experiences as they are happening is possible via the key to human consciousness: our ability to think, conceptualize, and manipulate abstract realities. We have rightly placed

---

* Credit for the term "apparent not-self" goes to the late Ramchandra Gandhi, grandson of Mahatma Gandhi, and a former teacher of mine.

much importance on our rational abilities. They are the direction of evolution, and they will only grow from here.

This experience is so powerful and so enticing that it has caused modern humanity to deny the importance of the actual experiential reality of modes of understanding and knowing that took place on prior evolutionary levels. Yet the I experience of a rock, plant, or animal, though non-cognitive, is just as real as ours and should be no more difficult to posit than the I experience of a human. As we shall experience in Part Three of the Handbook, only the nature of the I differs.

In the same way that a child in development must build on all their experiences on the way to becoming a fully actualized and developed adult, so must humankind recognize and build with our rational mind upon modes of understanding that predate our current way of knowing and being. Even though we have ceased to use them, these understandings are still within us. Other than injury to our fragile egos, why then should the idea that I experience life as an individual aspect of a single I AM awareness be too hard for us to handle?

We can all agree that most people don't live their lives thinking about consciousness and existence and the nature of ultimate reality. We spend our time focusing on how to survive in the world around us. Depending on our age, this can mean getting good grades, avoiding the bully next door, holding down a job, getting along with our mate, paying the bills, or not falling while getting out of the shower. Everyday life can be a difficult enough maze to navigate without getting into the more profound, more esoteric questions like, "Who is actually trying to survive in the world around me?" That, however, is the question we are now going to answer in greater depth.

Only by accepting the reality of both ends of the polarity we experience - individual I and universal I AM - can humanity fully develop its potential without self-destructing first.

The experience is simply that I am a unique aspect of the multi-dimensional I AM, encompassing both an inner-intuitive mind and outer-cognitive mind. This is the meeting point of science and religion, intellectual activity in the light of spiritual awareness. Knowing this is living in New Consciousness and the ultimate key to survival of the human species.

* * *

Meeting I to I

Even though you and I experience our personal I in the exact same way, it is still impossible, in English, for both of us to be I in the same sentence, or both be you for that matter. It all depends on who's speaking. When I say I, it means me, the writer of these words, as opposed to you, the reader of these words. Likewise, when I say you, it means you, the reader, as opposed to me, the writer. However, when you say I or you say you, it all gets reversed. The reference keeps changing depending on who is doing the speaking. That's just the way it goes. No wonder we feel we are looking at the world through separate Is.

This usage of I is in the structure of our language and, as a result, part of our mindset. And although it seems innocent enough, this is one of the very factors, spinal to our thought and awareness, that makes us think of ourselves as completely separate, disconnected individuals. And yes, though 'we' does mean the two of us, it's still the meeting of two separate Is.

Imagine, therefore, the difficulties that can occur when two people come together, as we are doing now, in an attempt to share the inner experiences we have in common. We must not only deal with multiple separate and distinct realities—yours, mine, and the one(s) in between— we've got to figure out a way to communicate these realities.

For example, let's say it's a beautiful morning, and our two Is are walking towards each other on a path in the park, and we smile and nod as we approach. Will we choose to stop and talk? Well, that depends.

Before the Handbook we probably wouldn't. We didn't know each other then and the only impetus to stop would have been a visual one, an external image reaching our senses from *out there*. My I would have seen you, your I would have seen this old guy, and there's a good chance that neither I would have considered the possibility of any kind of connection. Chances are we would have kept right on walking.

But now things are different. Even though the outer experience of facing each other is the same as before, that external reality now projects an inner meaning it didn't have previously. We've already been hanging out together for roughly ninety pages, and purely physical factors are not what would impel each I to stop. It's the ideas we know we can share that are of interest, the thoughts and concepts and landscapes of each other's inner worlds. The physical housing of those inner worlds isn't what's important anymore.

Now, I know I cannot know all about you, the history, the relationships, the personality, the urges in the heart, the knowings in the mind, the images flitting across the otherwise grey-black screen behind your eyes. I can take a stab at it, but I do not know all that. The question is whether what I do know about you is worth stopping to talk to or not. And that's true for your I as well.

I remember once walking barefoot on San Francisco's Ocean Beach. The sky was clear, the day was warm, and I stopped to take it all in. The sun was on my face, my eyes were closed, and my hands folded in a meditative position of receptivity. My eyes flickered open about ten minutes later just in time to see a young woman pass beyond my field of vision. A few moments later, before I had moved a muscle, a young man came trotting past in the same direction. Without missing a beat, he nodded towards me and recited a perfect impromptu haiku:

> *You are wise, old man*
> *But the girl that I follow*
> *Is much prettier.*

...and kept going. He clearly knew his priorities. But I digress.

Though I don't know the content of your inner reality, I do know that such a reality exists and that it consists of a theater constantly in motion containing images, thoughts, ideas, desires, memories, everything known, everyone known, all the experiences of life, all the places visited, all the lessons learned, all the things you can do, all the things you believe you cannot do. All of it is there in your unique inner reality. It's not all on the screen of your awareness at any one time, but it's all there to be accessed when needed, either in conscious awareness or in non-conscious reaction.

But enough of this standing around talking in the park. This I wants some breakfast and coffee. Do you want to stop and join me? Good.

* * *

Now visualize our Is in a diner having breakfast together, seated in a booth facing each other. In this particular setting, there are three realities we must deal with that will affect what we say, what we do, and how we relate to each other.

The first reality is in the outer world between us, the one in front of our eyes. Even though this is the world where scientific measurement is possible, and everything is supposed to be objective, we will not be experiencing it in exactly the same way. Certainly, we will see some things from the same perspective, such as the door we came in, the counter over there, and the server who keeps forgetting to bring a refill of coffee.

We will also see some things in reverse perspective, namely the items on the table between us, the menus, the silverware, the jelly jar, and the placemats.

There will also be some things only one of us can see, such as the face of the person we're talking to and the parts of the diner in front of us but out of the other's field of vision. This does not even take into account that our sets of eyes may not be equally as sharp, or that one of us may be somewhat more colorblind than the other. Plus, we haven't even started talking about potential differences in sensitivity to sounds and odors and tastes. Clearly, we will be experiencing our common outer-worldly experience together, but differently.

However, equally without question, we should be able to agree that all the inputs that we are experiencing in this diner are real, right?

The second reality is the one behind your eyes. It's external to me, but it's internal to you. It includes your name, your attributes, your likes and dislikes, your talents and abilities, where you work, where you head after work is done, and who's waiting for you when you get there. It includes all of the stuff we talked about in the park, everything and everyone in your history that makes you who you are today, whether you remember them or not. It's as unique to you as your DNA, and why you are who you are and why you ordered what you did. And lest there be any doubt, even though it cannot be weighed and measured, it's just as real to you as the outer world before your eyes.

I, of course, have a similar world behind my eyes that is just as real for me as yours is for you. That's why I go home to a different place than you do, and why I probably like different music, and why I ordered the corned beef hash, eggs, and black coffee, while you ordered whatever that is you're eating. Hey, there's no accounting for tastes, right?

On a more subtle level, I am naturally drawn to a physicality that reflects my inner reality just as you are drawn to a physicality that reflects yours. We each relate to the common outer world from a stance and perspective that marks our own unique inner world. Each I sees different elements in the same reality and relates to the same elements differently.

Pick-pockets look at the crowd passing them in a completely different way than the rest of us, while TV news commentators can replay something we both saw in common, explaining with their expertise something important that we missed. So even though it seems there should be experiential commonalities outside, what I experience in outer reality also turns out to be unique for each and every I.

Our shared external experience will be individually imprinted on the screens of our unique inner realities. As a result, tomorrow, when we think of what we experienced in common here today, it will be remembered differently for each of us, thereby affecting our interactions with other external experiences in the future.

At a later 'now' when we recall our meeting, our inner realities - comprised as they are of memories of the prior external 'now' experience - will not be the same. I could have noticed something you did not. You could remember something that I did not. One I could have enjoyed something the other I absolutely hated. Like this coffee. Doesn't it seem a little weak to you? Really? You think it's strong?

Does this mean that one of us interpreted the experience incorrectly or remembered the meeting incorrectly? Of course not. I would have to be extremely egotistical to think so. Each I simply imprints what is important in a way that is natural for them.

Clearly, our experience together is experienced separately by two independently operating units: the personal I and the universal I AM. We see this is true. We experience this is true. We know this is true, even though the prevailing paradigm to places validity only on the measurable, external elements of our meeting, rather than the experiential, internal ones. New Consciousness, however, does examine the internal experience that frames the content for each experiential I.

Back at the park when we stopped to talk and went to the diner, it was because each of us was impelled by a will from within our inner reality to halt the forward movement of the physical body. If either of us had not wanted to stop, both of us would still be walking. A neurophysiologist might say that it was the such-and-such chemical, or neuron, or electrical impulse that got the I to stop walking, and they would be correct, but only in the limited sense of looking at the physical body from the physical point of view.

On a deeper level, it was seeing you coming in the other direction that stirred up an inner, non-material desire that made me want to stop and talk, thus causing the such-and-such neuron to fire. At the very least, a reasonable neurophysiologist and I should be able to agree that both the physical and non-physical factors affecting my stopping are real and co-arising.

But enough talk. It's been fun sharing these thoughts with you over breakfast. Remember, don't take my word for anything. What's said here will be meaningful to you only as you feel it resonate with everything else you experience as real. Now, let's start using some of these skills and abilities you have discovered within yourself. And though we will ultimately be heading to the ends of the universe through time and space, we'll start off easily enough by having you come face to face with someone you know very well indeed. Finish your coffee, do the exercise, and how about leaving the tip.

* * *

I live inside my body...
here... inside...
inside the skin

Everything else is...
there... outside...
outside the skin

And that's what separates me and you...
I am inside... You are outside.

And you know exactly what I mean.
Cause it's the same for you.

When you say I and I say I...
We point in the same direction...

...inside...

So ultimately, If we work it right...
we should be able to see...

I to I

Evolution of Me Game

Part One

Walk over to a mirror. Look closely at the person looking back. Without making value judgments, ask yourself what that person has in common with you and how that person differs from you.

> (Seriously. Do it. Look at yourself in a mirror before reading further. Or, if you don't feel like getting up just now, close your eyes and visualize yourself looking in the mirror. Then, do the real mirror later. We're talking experientially here, and as you already know, reading may allow you to learn about the subject, but you will not *know* the subject. Knowing, as we all know by now, is internal.)

At first glance, the person in the mirror appears to be exactly the same as I am - the one doing this exercise. That being is the same sex and age as I am, has my color hair and my color eyes, is wearing the same clothing as me, and has the same expression on their face that I have on mine. In fact, every external thing about the two of us is exactly the same, except for an interesting transposition of left and right. Any scars, birthmarks, or bandages on my face or body are on the other side. If I am right-handed, they are left-handed, if I am left-handed, they are right-handed.

This transposed image, of course, is not surprising; it's how I have been viewing me for as long as I can remember. However, and this is very interesting, I am the only one in the world who sees me this way, since I am the only one in the world who needs a mirror to see my face, to see the way I look from the outside. I wonder what that means? I never thought about it before.

However, there is another special relationship I have with the I in the mirror that no one else has or could ever have. We both live in the same here and now. Everything I am experiencing, that person is experiencing too. Not only that, I also know what exists in their inner reality because it is exactly the same as what exists in mine.

That person has the same talents, skills, likes and dislikes as I do and the exact same views on political issues, taste in music, art, movies, and books. They are involved in the same relationships, do the same work, have the same hobbies, the same habits, both good and bad, and the same dreams and aspirations. As far as inner reality goes, we're really one of a kind.

Now, become the person in the mirror and look back at yourself. It should be easy, right? After all, you are exactly the same, except for that left/right transposition. Interesting, isn't it? Looking at each other from either direction, you can truly say, "We really do see I to I."

* * *

Part Two

Get a photograph of yourself as a child. Look closely at the person looking back. Without making value judgments, ask yourself what that person has in common with you and how that person differs from you.

There are, of course, a lot of similarities between the two of us, although there's most certainly not the exact physical replication I experienced a moment ago while looking in the mirror. True, there was a point in space/time when the match was exact, but that's no longer the case. I may be taller or fatter now or have hair of a different color or less of it. Birthmarks may still show, but scars and bandages might not. However, that mirroring transposition between left and right is missing. I am looking at that younger me from the outside, just like everyone else. I wonder what that means?

There are other differences between the two of us that cannot be seen in the picture: differences in our inner reality. This was not always the case. There was a 'now' when I shared an inner reality with the I in the photo just as I do now with the I in the mirror. That's when their thoughts, talents, skills, abilities, and dreams were my thoughts, talents, skills, abilities and dreams.

Though I no longer look like the I in the photo, by traveling my inner memory to the 'now' of that image, a trip made possible since I was there when that picture was taken, I can access the inner reality of what I felt like, knew, and experienced when I looked like that. "If I only knew then what I know now" may not be a possibility, but the inverse is. I can know now what I knew then. And so, I begin my inner journey.

I start by removing from the inner reality of the I in the photo the names and the faces of people I have met since then, the places I moved and the books I have read. I eliminate one by one, the experiences and knowings I have had since that picture was taken. As I do that, step by step, I return in my 'now' to the I that I was in an earlier experiential time and space.

Depending on our age differences, the amount of inner knowing to be removed from 'now' will vary. That younger me may not have my education and may not know the person of my most intimate current relationship. They will not see the pictures in their inner reality of the experiences I have had since the picture I am now looking at was taken.

Our likes and dislikes may be the same, or not. "When did I begin to like asparagus?" Little by little, I can remove those things about me that the previous I did not have, did not know. Was that experience that changed my life part of the I of the picture, or was it still unknown, waiting to reveal itself to a future I?

The farther back the photo, the greater the difference in inner reality between the I of today and the I in the image. Ultimately, if I look at a photo of myself as an infant, I don't even know my name, nor how to care for myself or survive in the world. My inner reality is close to a blank, unless you believe in reincarnation, but that's another story.

In that picture of me in the hospital, wrinkled skin, eyes closed, held by the mother I so recently left, I may not even know that I am a separate being. I may not even know there is an *out there*. I may not even know there is an *in here*. I may not even know I am, or maybe I do, but isn't that what we're ultimately trying to find out?

Stop for a moment. Take a break. It's not that easy at first to go inside and look around. Focus on *out there* for a moment. Relax.

While we're out here, take a deep breath and look at what each and every I who played these last few games just experienced. The details are subjective, but the core experience is the same.

As I played the game, moving back and forth between experiencing myself now and experiencing myself as a child, anyone looking at me from the outside would have thought I was here in my body, the same as usual. But inside, in my mind, when I really got into it and remembered how I felt back in the photo, I was able to experience 'there and then' as 'here and now' without skipping a beat.

How did I do that? Was I existing in two different points in space/time at once? Or did I go back and forth between them? If so, was one of those points 'inside' me and the other 'outside' me? Does it even matter? I did it. And no matter where I was, my feeling of being me was exactly the same.

Really, that's the key. The movement in awareness and consciousness from there to now, from then to here, is a continuum even though it is instantaneous. It is a common experience that is traceable for each and every I, despite differences in content. It is also the evolutionary flow and the key to heading back through our individual event horizons to the very start of the universe and every point along the way.

* * *

Part Three

In your mind, visualize yourself in a future 'now' as the I you most want to be. Be in that present moment. Ask yourself, "How did I get here?" Then ask yourself if the current continuum is leading to that goal, and if it isn't, you are free to make a mid-course correction. Then go for it.

However, you must place your future vision in the setting you most want it to be, relate it to where you are now, and trace the steps that got you there from here. If you follow that path it will actually be the greatest possible use of your talents and skills and what you were truly designed for in the first place.

(Okay. This part is optional, and you could actually play without having played the first two levels. But you'd get it all wrong. You'd just be wishing and hoping instead of visualizing and manifesting. It's all about the experience, remember? *Being*, not doing.)

Light Upon the Water

Go down to the beach some night when the moon is full over the water, and you'll experience a common inner reality in the light of a unique outer reality. By the way, if you really want a different perspective on things, don't think of the moon as "The Moon". Sure, that's what we call it, but when we do that, it's just "The Moon", up in the sky where it's supposed to be. Instead, think of it, visualize it, feel it without a name as what it is: a huge ball of solid rock hanging there in space above your head. See if that doesn't give you a little extra appreciation for the laws of physics.

Once the "wow moment" passes, look up at the rock and enjoy its presence. Note the ways you experience its light. There is the focused intensity directly lighting its face and the diffused lightness it radiates in the general darkness, the field of moon shadows. Then there is the reflection of moonlight on the water, a shimmering dancing streak of light coming directly from the moon to you, through your eyes, and only your eyes. It must be coming directly to you, for on either side of this band of light connecting you and the moon, you see only darkness.

Logically, this raises a question. Since a particular location on the water is only lit when I look at the moon from a particular place on the shore, am I seeing an actual reflection on the water, or is this just something going on in my mind? The person over there cannot see the reflection connection between the moon and me. That person sees their own moon reflection, something I cannot see, although I know it must exist since the two of us are not different physiologically. We each have our eye, we each have our I, and we each have our individual streak of moonlight.

Now, walk on the beach, and an even more amazing process occurs. The light follows, staying with your I wherever you go. I am in the spotlight at every single moment, so to speak. As before, on either side there are no rays, even where there had been one just a moment before when I was standing there and saw it. The potential for that space being lit is still there, of course, as it will be as soon as some other I stands there. In fact, if enough people stand next to each other facing the moon, in theory, the entire arc of the beach will be lit, though each I will see only their own little part.

This way of seeing the moon is a common physiological experience crossing age, gender, racial, national, ethnic, religious, language, and even species lines. Long have beings looked out over the water and seen a reflection of the moon coming right toward them as we do. We are not the first to reflect on the reflection.

So, here's the question: Is this interaction between I, the moon, and the light waves bouncing off the water going on inside my head in my inner reality, or *out there* in my outer reality? If it's *out there*, my experience should be visible by others, which it isn't. If it's *in here* then it's not something physical, though it's very, very, real.

It's so real, in fact, that cameras record moonlight on water just as I do. Put a camera on a tripod facing the moon, walk down the beach, take a snapshot with a remote control, and you'll record a picture of a reality nobody saw even as it was happening, nobody but the camera.

I'm sure there are scientists who can explain what's happening. As for me, a mere philosopher and phenomenologist, it simply seems as if I have some part in the process of creating light ripples on the water, that the light appears because I am looking. That's exciting.

Part Three:

Earth and Evolution

* * *

I AM is what I AM

...a singular reality...
...pervading the universe...
...source of all human consciousness...

...and therefore...

...foundation of both science and religion.

* * *

Science/Religion and New Consciousness

Within the history of Western thought, there has long existed an ongoing either/or conflict between adherents of two polar complementary positions, the religious worldview and scientific worldview. Science teaches that reality is all outside and measurable. Religion preaches that it is all inside and mystical. Since the realm of each falls outside the set of basic premises encompassed by the other, a common meeting point is not possible without additional input, inclusive of both positions. New Consciousness, the explanation of reality proposed here, provides such a perspective and forms the framework for resolving this age-old confrontation.

We have already discovered that reality is both inside and outside, making each one of us the bridge between two different experiential dimensions: non-manifest consciousness and unconscious manifestation. It is through our own awareness, our own experience, our own consciousness and the individual experience of I, that the theory and actions of both science and religion – outside and inside – are unified into the single activity of being. Simply being.

Of course, many philosophers and prophets, particularly Eastern and Indigenous masters, have been saying for millennia that pure Consciousness, the I AM experience, is the source of who we are and the origin of it all. The ancient Indian teachings of Kashmir Shaivism, for example, dating back to 3000 B.C., call this Oneness, Sat-chit-ānanda, three Sanskrit words that translate as Existence-Consciousness-Bliss, a view paralleled by the modern teachings of Siddha Yoga and the Integral philosophy of Sri Aurobindo. Native American teachings also tell of the Oneness. Unfortunately, these teachings have been drowned out by cultures where competition and possession are more important than cooperation and sharing.

Even in Western theology, when Moses asks God for his name, and he responds, "I AM that I AM" (Exodus 3:14), that would seem to come to the same conclusion. Similarly, Jesus' words, *"the kingdom of heaven is within you"* (Luke 17:21), could not be more to the point. Plus, Jesus' words that have been translated from Aramaic as *"I am the way"* (John 14:6) could just as easily have been translated as "I am *is* the way." And that simple and factual change in how ancient Aramaic was translated many centuries ago brings Christianity and New Consciousness into agreement.

While Newtonian physics has steadily railed against any reality that cannot be measured and quantified, solutions to the basic questions have not been forthcoming from such scientific materialism. Enter quantum physics with its theoretical assumptions positing "dark matter" and "dark energy" as non-physical forces affecting manifested reality. The door has been opened.

However, there are still some members of the scientific community who would object to what we are doing here because it goes against mainstream beliefs or because no mathematical proof is provided. To them, I say, try it before you object. A spherical Earth goes against a flat Earth. Quantum physics goes against Newtonian physics. Intuitive enlightenment goes against old ways of thinking and always has. I say it again: if you cannot open your mind to new possibilities and new ways of thinking, are you really a scientist?

It is true, I am not a mathematician. I am a phenomenologist. I can merely take you to places you have not been to before and show you sights and give you feelings that will open up infinite possibilities and excite your minds. I leave it to you to juggle the numbers and create the equations. Note that nothing said here goes against any measurements or findings of modern quantum theory. Quantum physicists are the ones who have related non-material waves and material particles. They are the ones who have said that some things exist depending on whether we are looking at them or not. They are the ones who are now saying that it appears that the observer is creating the observed.

Those scientists willing to apply New Consciousness to their work will discover the Grand Unification Theory they have long been seeking. They will find a common binding factor underlying everything. Once it is seen, the entire body of already existing scientific research becomes subject to whole new interpretations without changing any of the factual results of that research. How fascinating. Simply by looking at the same results from a different perspective, information and findings already available will lead to new understandings.

Such controlled experimentation, falling outside the scope of the Handbook, are simple, rational, inexpensive, and applicable to any particularized field, requiring only the application of New Consciousness to work that has already been done. That, plus a recognition that consciousness is a process more than an object and that any externally oriented approach cannot help but be limited to a partial understanding of the totality. Just as Copernicus did almost 500 years ago, consciousness awaits a scientific explanation of its material unfolding by an imaginative thinker who can look at the sun moving across the heavens and see Earth rotating.

Similarly, by bringing science into the equation, New Consciousness will allow religion to experience validation of an ultimately omnipotent presence and source of all. It will provide insight into the words of the various prophets that this source is not external but exists within each and every one of us. God, called by whatever name you wish to use, is not an unreachable supernatural external being but the underlying energy common to us all and the actual source of our very existence. Might widespread knowledge of this universal truth lead to a spiritual renaissance and an ending of sectarian conflict between religious factions? We can certainly hope this is the case. You can never tell with humans.

While we wait for science and religion to catch up, it's not necessary for individuals to remain at arm's length when talking about New Consciousness and applying its principles of unified reality. Rather, we can participate in the actual, subjective, inner/outer experience of that unified reality in all its diversity, including those polar complementary positions that appear antithetical to the entrenched opposing disciplines.

Ultimately, each of us must undertake our own shift of consciousness, the collective shift being a composite of the sum of the parts. This means that ideals must be made manifest and new platforms of awareness reached. Yet to date we continue to speak about shifts in consciousness from within the old consciousness. Action is required. Theory must become practice. We must walk the talk. The paradigm must shift. It's all voluntary from this point on, remember?

The Handbook is designed to bridge the gap between intellect and intuition, scientific and spiritual, theory and practice for each and every one of us. In so doing we are attempting to manifest the ideal rather than merely writing about it. So, take that step. Feeling connected to the Oneness changes everything, and you are invited to be a part of the evolution. And since you have gotten this far and are reading this sentence, there's a good chance you are already well on your way. Thank you. And welcome to the future.

* * *

Now The Real Fun Begins

If you have played all the games and done all the exercises you've run into on the path thus far, you should have already accomplished quite a bit while traveling the evolutionary road to New Consciousness.

You've discovered that your very self-awareness and feeling of existence wasn't necessarily created by your brain, but may have been received by your brain from an original and universal source of consciousness. In which case, even though you are an absolutely unique individual, different from any other creature who ever has, currently does, or ever will exist, your very feeling of existence is the same feeling of existence experienced by every creature in the universe. And that led to the awareness that every creature in the universe is living, whether they are evolved enough to know it or not.

You have learned that according to this new paradigm, the consciousness you feel inside is the same consciousness we all feel inside. Not "the same as", but "the absolute same consciousness". Furthermore, this feeling of consciousness with which we are all so familiar is the absolute foundation of the universe. It is the God of religion, the singularity of modern science, whatever you want to call it. This means that all those special characteristics about you that make you one of a kind are adjectives and filters surrounding the universal I AM and are ultimately designed to be used for the greater good.

You have been made aware of the difference between your inside and your outside, recognized the difference between I and 'apparent not-I' and begun to pay attention to where you are focusing your attention. In doing so, you have recognized that both the inside world and the outside world are real and affect your actual experiential life, since your I exists at the synapse where the world of inner meaning and the world of outer measurement come together.

You have also practiced traveling back to your earlier days in this lifetime, a voyage made possible because the I of that different being, time, and reality is the very same I that you are using today. The key, it turns out, is not trying to experience other beings from the outside in, but from the inside out.

Now, having done all of that, we are ready to dive in head first, so to speak. Doing nothing you have not already done, but merely focusing your I a little farther away from where you are now, you are going to ride consciousness back to the beginning of life on Earth. And if that's not enough, in Part Four of the Handbook, we are going to make the quantum leap back to the very start of the universe to learn how it all began.

But one thing at a time. Join me as we head back through time, space, and experiential reality to the point where life on Earth began. Hold on, it should be a fun and enlightening trip.

* * *

The Only Constant is Change

The material world is a process undergoing constant continuums of change. A rose, for example, does not suddenly burst on the scene as a totally open and vibrant beauty. There is a thickening of the stem, a swelling, a budding, an opening, a spreading, a sending of scent, a visiting by bees, a wilting, a dying.

Each "now", as we look at the rose, is different than it was just a moment before, in an earlier "now". And if the changes are too subtle for us to register with our human eye, stop-action cameras can compress the process in time, so we can see the continuous movement of the different stages of rose.

Similarly, a building being constructed goes through a continuum of different stages prior to occupancy and use. There's the hole in the ground, foundation, framing, siding, roofing, interior design, and landscaping, each a part of the process of the reality of the building. And that's not even including the financing, architectural drawings, zoning permits, building permits, and all the other early-on elements necessary to construct a building that aren't visible to the casual observer. Once construction reaches the physical stage, it's easy to see the step-by-step process taking place as it's happening. However, the process is actually underway once the idea for that building arises in someone's mind, quite real in their inner reality but unseen in the outer world, or anyone else's inner reality for that matter.

Continuums occur in technology, the Wright brothers' flyer of 1903 becoming modern supersonic transports, laptop computers and iPhones of today having greater capacity and capability than room-sized computers of the 1960's. Continuums exist in social and cultural realms as well. Economic systems expand and complexify, styles of music and art develop, and civilizations rise and fall. What's present today wasn't here yesterday and won't be here tomorrow, at least in the same form as today. Recognizing continuums and experiencing where things were and where things are is important in allowing us to take an educated guess at where things will be in some future 'now'.

Only one thing is certain. Everything we view as a snapshot in a particular 'now' can be seen not just as a static fact of reality, the way it "is", but as a moment along a constantly evolving process which grew, somehow or other, out of what came before and will lead, somehow or other, to what comes next. Change and evolution are the static quality of the process of outer, physical reality.

Consciousness, too, as it manifests within creatures of the physical world, is subject to change in a natural process continuum of growth and evolution. In the same way that evolution occurs in the outer world of beings, measurable by biologists, anthropologists, and archeologists, evolution occurs in the inner world of beings. And it's just as capable of being examined by anyone, such as yourself, who knows how to use their inner I.

Even though we know as fact that Earth has been evolving for millions of years and humans haven't always been on board, it's not part of our natural thought process to realize this means that once upon a time, rocks were probably the most complex and advanced beings around. And although plants don't represent the most evolved and complex creatures existing on the planet today, there can be no question of the great evolutionary breakthrough that occurred when that form of life first hit the scene. If nothing else, just look at all the many things plants can do that rocks can't. Similarly, animal life and human life each brought the level of complexity as manifested on Earth to new and hitherto unimagined heights.

Human capabilities are so far above and beyond the levels and capacities of the life forms that once dominated Earth that we tend to consider ourselves the ultimate development of evolution just as we are. With only a recent and cursory nod in the direction of whales, dolphins, and elephants, we believe our experience of conscious reality to be the highest evolution of brain and mind possible. Some have even referred to humans as the goal of all creation.

Surprise!

Despite our protests to the contrary and even our acceptance that we might be the highest development consciousness has yet produced on Earth, there's no reason to assume that evolution has come to a grinding halt with us exactly as we are. For just as ever-increasing conscious awareness evolved in a continuum through the physical forms of mineral, vegetable, animal, and human, so is New Consciousness continuing the evolutionary process.

Ultimately, the I experience arises from the two ends of the spectrum - outer non-aware materiality and inner non-material awareness - coming together. It must be this way since meaningless matter does not have nor experience an inner world, and matterless meaning does not have nor experience an outer world. Since both are needed for Self-awareness, I show up at the synapse where they meet. How else could it be?

As a result of the experiential human ability to be aware of one's own inner and outer realities at the same time (something I hope you didn't gloss over in Part Two of the Handbook), we can now use New Consciousness and the process of phenomenology to examine the universal evolution of consciousness. Without losing the awareness of who I am as a conscious, self-aware, thinking being, I can actually retrace the path consciousness has taken in its emergence into the physical reality of "now".

The technique you will use is the exact same one you used when you looked at a photograph of your younger self and retraced the evolution of your individual I from "now" back to then. You are just going to be using your more universal I, working within your own mind, looking at what it's doing at any moment, subtracting out anything that could not have occurred in the I of an earlier conscious being. Simply by watching yourself as you clear your mind of everything that the earlier conscious being could not have experienced — poof! There I am, and here I am, too, watching as it happens.

I need only witness what I experience as I am experiencing it and recognize whether my focus is inside or outside. And that's something I already know I am able to do.

Before setting out across this synapse between my current consciousness and pre-human consciousness, we should make certain that the places we intend to go actually exist. I'd hate to have some scientist say that what we're doing here isn't real. So, we will borrow the image of a rope bridge swinging high above a canyon floor. And, like any good adventurer, before stepping out onto the bridge, we should make sure that both ends are firmly set in place.

* * *

Supposition One: Conscious Beings Currently Exist

This is a rock-solid starting point of agreement since I, the being "now" reading these words, both exist and am conscious, no matter how I wish to define it. I have to be conscious to be reading this, and so I can say with absolute conviction that I ...

this is true. I am aware. I am conscious. I am. Conscious beings currently exist.

* * *

Supposition Two: Non-Conscious Beings Currently Exist

There should be no disagreement here either, for this is the basis of the scientific paradigm. Try to get some scientist to say that rocks have consciousness, indeed! New Consciousness might not totally agree with that, but it would concur experientially that whatever self-awareness and cognitive capabilities were used one paragraph ago to define me as being conscious, there are beings and forms that do not have those same capabilities, such as rocks. In other words, it is clear that not every being exhibits inner self-awareness nor has an equal ability to either consciously or non-consciously react with their external environment as I do. New Consciousness and the current paradigm can at least agree on that.

* * *

Supposition Three: The Direction of Evolution is Toward Ever More Complex Levels and Expressions of Consciousness

While conscious and non-conscious beings, as science defines them, presently coexist on Earth, the continuum of change appears to be in the direction of complexification of consciousness rather than simplification. Thus, it is logical to state that there was a time on Earth when the most evolved creatures were not as aware of their own consciousness as humans are now. So given these three points of grounding, we can begin the retracing of consciousness on Earth.

* * *

There Had To Be A First Time

If something didn't always exist and now does, there had to be a first time when it did, or was. And that includes experiences. Within the Western paradigm of linear time, there has to be a time when any characteristic or capability that differentiates a given experience from all other experiences first took place.

We are familiar with this ourselves as individuals. For anyone who drives a car, there had to be a first time that you drove a car. Or, since infants do not read books and 'now' you are reading this one, there had to be a first time you read a book, etc. Similarly, on a larger scale, since humans did not always drive cars and 'now' they do, there had to be a first time when a car was driven, and a first time when a book was read.

If, once upon a time, the total reality of Earth did not include characteristics and capabilities that can be defined as the self-conscious experience, and now the total reality of Earth does include those experiences, then at some point, there had to be a 'first' experience which we, looking back from our evolved perspective, would consider to be indicative of self-consciousness.

As I head back to that point of experience, there should be no difference between the levels of consciousness I have put on over the eons to get to where I am now and the levels of consciousness I will be taking off as I retrace those steps. The only difference is that this time around I can watch while it happens.

As we prepare for our journey, I caution against falling into the trap of questioning how many millions of years ago any of the particulars we shall be experiencing took place. Similarly, it's important not to get concerned with what the being that first had any particular conscious experience looked like, or was named, or even which experience crossed over the line between what we call mineral, plant, animal, and human. New Consciousness posits an evolutionary continuum that uses fixed categories only as prototypical examples of consciousness levels for comparison purposes, similar to the way that quantum physics only examines waves by stopping them long enough to allow for their observation as a particle.

Besides, knowledge of names is not knowledge of an experience, and the experience itself exists, irrespective of how humans talk about it. The I experience is neither dependent on the external appearance of the being having that experience nor the name we give it. Precognitive states of consciousness cannot be replicated within a framework that includes cognitive constructions that the experiencer couldn't have had.

Such thinking leads nowhere but more definitions, giving the flavor of having subsumed knowledge without yielding any actual nutrition. From our cognitive viewpoint, it might be fun to know, but information like that is similar to knowing the words inside and outside without being the box and actually experiencing an inside and an outside. It's knowing about an experience without really having the experience. The more meaningful exercise undertaken here is to apply phenomenology and personally experience the knowing of that first self-consciousness being as it happens.

As we experience the mindset of our emergent predecessors, only a portion of our inner reality will become as numb and blank as theirs, not our awareness of it, a capability they did not have. Our I will remain present, in two awarenesses. Think of that. Only evolved, self-aware beings could go on the fantastic voyage we are about to take, experiencing another being's consciousness while retaining our own. This technique is both the cornerstone of the emerging field of pragmatic phenomenology and an indication of the evolutionary level already reached by the human mind. Its use allows replicable experiential knowing at all points along the conscious continuum. How fun is that?

But, enough talking about it. That only produces questions that exist within circles of not knowing, and our enquiring minds want to know. It's time for action, time to take the next step in the search for consciousness. It's time to play a game.

* * *

* * *

Just imagine...
The first time some being felt...
'I am'
the feeling of being separate...
from out there.

Just imagine...
The first time some being felt...
'I AM'
the feeling of not being separate...
from out there.

What a difference!

Retracing Evolution: The Trek Begins

So, here's the plan. You are going to use the skills you've already picked up in playing these experiential mind games and mental exercises to place your awareness somewhere deep inside of yourself where you can experience two different realities at once. You did it earlier when you looked at the photo of your younger self and saw that person from the outside while experiencing them from the inside at the same time. Remember?

This time you're going to send your mind back to the early days of Earth as a non-knowing, non-aware being. At the same time, you are going to experience pure non-material consciousness, God Consciousness, if you want to call it that, and watch what happens as that being experiences the first flush of individual consciousness, the first experience of self-aware I. Your own personal I is going to be the pivot point of the two. This is something you should be getting good at by now.

Find a nice, quiet place to sit and turn off your phone and any other electronic devices. You're going to go deep inside, and the less interruptions the better. As you prepare to experience the emergence of consciousness, you note that if, along the way, you find some external reality that defies the principle of New Consciousness, then the whole concept is blown out of the water. If you do not, then what you're about to experience might just be the way it actually happened. But why get ahead of yourself? "Strap in," you say, smiling and revving the engines.

Since the purpose of this experiment is to experience the first blush of self-aware consciousness, you need to go far enough back in time to take up station in a material body that does not have conscious I awareness of itself. Once you do, as the fully conscious being you currently are, you will be able to watch what happens when the two of you meet for the very first time.

You begin by taking all thoughts, ideas, beliefs, speculations, suppositions, opinions, prejudices, observations, and other assorted mental fabrications and removing them from that part of your mind that is heading back in time. You must forget about computers, television, taxes, airplanes, automobiles, houses, cholesterol, music, money, clothing, politics, and on and on and on.

These must obviously be eliminated from your mind, along with every other creation of human society. The first being to experience consciousness wasn't concerned with the details of modern living that occupy our minds. Should any such ideas, concepts, or constructions arise that you know couldn't have preceded the primal I experience we are seeking, simply strike it from what that being you are sending back has in mind, even though you will retain it in yours. It's the same thing you did when you removed knowledge currently in your mind from the mind of the photo of you as a child.

Even the idea of basic survival must go, an experience not just valid for people living today but real for those who existed hundreds and thousands of years ago, in ancient Greece, China, and Africa, in cities, in huts, and in caves. Though the content of outer reality is different for all of these points in space/time, as long as there's an inner awareness of the simplest, most primitive concerns for personal survival, there must already be a concept of self, an awareness that I am. After all, who is it who wants to survive, if not I? You are going back before that.

Language will cease to exist. Sounds are one thing, up to a point, but words are characteristic of advanced rational beings already possessing basic self-awareness, able to give meaning to vibrations moving from outer reality to inner reality. You must also stop the use of reason and logic. You simply will not have the brain/mind for it.

You must lose all conception of past and future, as well as all worry for what might happen, and all regret for what did. As you head backward towards the unfolding of consciousness, you must forget that you have a physical body. To know I have anything means to know that I am, and once you know that, it's too late to know what it was like prior to knowing that.

The being you are becoming in your mind is becoming non-responsive. You look at its inner reality and realize why you're losing contact. There's not much grey matter there to hold onto and you don't want to go too far and deconstruct yourself back beyond the physical. The point in space/time you're looking to experience is that initial awareness of yourself as a physical being, separate and distinct from the surrounding environment, a recognition that arises with the awareness of the difference between self and other. In fact, that's the only way one can be consciously aware of oneself as a separate being - if there's also an awareness of another, an apparent not-self. Without recognition of "not-I", I cannot exist as a separate I. But you already know that. Therefore, you will experience the origin of embodied consciousness, with the simple binary distinction between inner and outer, between me and something else.

However, to have that first experience and find out what it feels like as it's happening, you must go back even farther. Once something is in your brain/mind, as you recall, it's too late to find out either where it came from or to share the original experience. Isn't it amazing how conscious experiences span space and time?

A siren and warning light suddenly go off in your mind, and you realize that you haven't been paying close attention to where you are in time. You check all channels and realize you're not getting any feedback at all from your inner self. You stop the regression and look around, but all you see are a bunch of rocks.

* * *

Solid Like a Rock

So, what's the inner 'I' consciousness of a rock, once the highest, most advanced form of being on Earth? From the outside, it is pretty hard to tell.

What can we observe for starters? Well, rocks do interact in numerous ways with the outer world around them. They're subject to the force of gravity and are worn away by the constant friction of running water. If there's too much pressure on them, they crumble or fuse or turn into diamonds if they happen to be made of carbon. If there's too much heat on them, they melt. But in all of these interactions, they seem to be passive.

Rocks don't display any form of activity that would seem to demonstrate an internal I awareness of what's going on around them. This is what you'd expect, of course, since there's nothing inside of them resembling a "brain". Their physical insides are the same as their physical outsides. Clearly, their synapse in the physical, material world seems to exist on their surface, between the rock and everything else. They appear to have no awareness of an inner I.

As a result, rocks display no interest in their environment nor their future and no desire, conscious or non-conscious, to change or improve their existence. At least, that is the way it appears from the outside. Put them in one place and they sit there, well, like a rock, unless, of course, they're acted upon. But even then, it doesn't appear that rocks have any idea of what's going on, certainly not as an individual I separate from other rocks. Such capabilities were still a number of evolutionary levels away when rocks were the leading edge of Earth consciousness. That's why rocks make lousy pets, despite marketing efforts to the contrary.

Yet rocks do affect the reality of all who come into contact with them by their mere presence and their solidity. Big ones like the Himalayas immediately come to mind. Indeed, that attribute of solidity is the inner reality of every boulder and stone you have ever climbed in your life. A rock, by its very weight, affects whatever happens to be underneath it at the time, while its presence allows it to be used by other more evolved beings for shade, shelter, art, industry, and religion.

More germane to our adventure, however, is the question of what inner awareness exists for an individual rock. Does it even have one?

While it's an observable fact that a rock doesn't seem to be aware of its relationships, and in that sense doesn't display what we would call consciousness, there could be two possible reasons for that. One is that rocks do not house consciousness. This is the view of the current paradigm. The other is that rocks house consciousness but are not able to experience and demonstrate it in a way that we can measure. This is the view of New Consciousness. Is there any way we can prove which view is correct? In a word, no. Consciousness only manifests through the capabilities of its possessor, and rocks do not have many capabilities.

True, there is much physical evidence to support the "nobody home" theory of rocks. Even if a falling rock crushes something underneath it, it's clear that gravity worked on the rock first, something that's always true when looking at what initiated any measurable movement for a rock. It can always be traced to an external source. In other words, rocks never make the first move, always sit still unless moved, and only go where they are prodded. These attributes of rocks are perfectly consistent with Newton's first two laws of physics.

On the other hand, if consciousness is permeating a rock, if a rock houses an I, what is that experience like? What would you, as a rock, be experiencing right now? You have no evolved organs of sensation; you cannot see, move, hear, taste, or smell. How, then, can you be aware of an outside reality when you do not possess the senses necessary for that to happen?

You can still have an inner reality. A rock can possess a feeling of solidity deep in its cells, not to think about but to experience, a wave length resonating that defines it as rock. Yet without the knowledge of outer reality, there can be no feeling of ego, of I as a special kind of rock, or a separate and unique rock among its own kind. It cannot know itself as a singular pebble, separate stone, or unique boulder. If the rock experiences anything, it's pure rockiness.

It seems to be a rule of thumb for scientists to say that a thing has to be able to roll in its own direction for it to be considered to be conscious, to have life. We cannot measure that capability in rocks and so we say rocks do not have it, even though we know from New Consciousness that the fact that we cannot measure something is no proof that it doesn't exist. It is an interesting metaphor, however, that where technology can measure change in radioactive rock, they say it has a "half-life". And what about crystals that actually do grow? Could it mean...? You store that thought in your mind and return to basics.

Rock is so deeply embedded in a cellular awareness, transcending individuality, that it cannot be described in any meaningful human terms as being aware of its own consciousness. You, as well, looking at rock from the outside...

that a rock, not knowing inside from outside, cannot know itself as different from others. That means that the rock doesn't possess individual I consciousness. So, if you want to refer to the rock as it, the English third-person pronoun that does not imply life, go right ahead. You won't be hurting anyone's feelings, especially the rock. Clearly, you have definitely traveled far enough back in time to predate individual consciousness. Realizing you have to move on in your quest, you pick up a rock to bring back as a souvenir. Visions of Neal Armstrong on the moon come to mind.

Growing Like a Plant

You jump forward in time, readjust your focus, and see a field of green, mirroring a new mood on the face of Earth, so different from what just was. Look around. There's no denying, the I experience of plants is a qualitative evolutionary step beyond rocks. Plants don't just react in response to their external environment. They initiate action on their own, modifying themselves in response to an energy that exists inside of them. That's something rocks just aren't capable of doing.

The fact that plants actively interact with their outer reality for their own ultimate purposes means that they do have an inner reality. The synapse between inner and outer occurs within the plant and not on the surface, although, like rocks, they are not aware that they have it.

Leaves turn to face the sun, growing roots split apart rock as they reach for water, vines strangle other plants, some plants even devour insects. There's something inherent in plants that acts upon the external world, some non-measurable inner reality that manifests through the plant, whether the individual plant is aware of it or not. While it's true that it's the fly who triggers the leaf to close, there has to be some individuality within that particular species of plant that co-arises with the fly-foot triggering. If not, every leaf the fly stepped on would close around it, not just those of the Venus flytrap.

Such energy, manifesting change from the inside-out, we call "life", and is the point where immeasurable inner process begins to affect measurable outer environment. This isn't to say, however, that any given plant is aware of interacting with the world around it. Indeed, even though plants demonstrate what we call life, this is where terminology determines whether we call the plant conscious or not.

From its very first stirrings, a plant will do its best to keep changing, to continue manifesting life. Unlike rocks, solidity is not a plant's long suit. Though dry plant seeds can lie dormant for centuries, once awakened by water, they become addicted to it, so to speak. Water doesn't want the plant, need the plant, nor seek it out, however desperately the plant might need the water.

Like consciousness, water doesn't care whether the plant knows it's there or not. The plant must reach out to the water to survive, and whether this plant or that plant survives, it's all the same to the water, life-sustaining source that it is. We know, by the way, that water is life-sustaining and not life-creating, because water does not spontaneously generate plants in all locations, only where there are seeds.

Just as the process of knowing is the same, regardless of the content of knowing, the process of physical development in initiating interaction with the environment is common for all plants, even though each plant interacts with external reality in its own unique and particular way. That's why there's such a vast profusion of plant life, capable of existing and surviving under the wide variety of external conditions found on the planet.

The fact that a plant initiates action in response to its external environment means that there must be some activity taking place "within" the plant. Clearly, initiation of action indicates a direction from inside-out, demonstrating some "inner reality" other than just the existence of an embedded physical subcomponent that is only capable of participating in interaction from the outside-in, as in rocks. The plant may not be able to talk about it, may not know it's there, but we know that something is going on inside just by observing.

It is clear, for example, that a rosebush experiences its I differently than a rock. As a rosebush, it brings a unique inner energy to its relationship with the outside, and given a hospitable environment, will spend all its energy fulfilling its nature as a rose bush. It will initiate movement by holding onto the soil and reaching for water with its roots while stretching upwards and outwards towards the light with its branches and leaves. It will grow and bloom and do the 'rose thing' to the best of its ability without any sort of developed self-aware ego sense, as experienced at the human level. The rosebush, after all, still does not have what we would call a brain.

Under the most favorable outer circumstances, the rosebush will bloom and blossom and grow and flourish to the maximum of its inner innate capacity. Should conditions be less than perfect - the soil devoid of nutrients, moisture minimal, a wall blocking light, or noxious gases stifling its pores - it will still hold the soil and reach for water and light in the best way it can, even though root length and leaf size will be small and there may or may not be enough energy left for buds and flowers.

Though any given rosebush may not appear as beautiful or shapely as others or grow and bloom as well as it would have grown had conditions been better, it certainly does not feel bad about its appearance. And, since it has no idea of I as an individual bush, there is no concern for how well I am or am not doing relative to the neighboring bushes. That would require an awareness of other rose bushes and what they are achieving, a capability that was several conscious levels away when plants were at the top of the evolutionary heap. Nor can there be any sort of self-awareness related to any specific parts or functions. There is absolutely nothing to indicate that a particular rosebush knows how its leaves are doing, or its thorns, or its flowers.

The plant simply does what it does in order to survive, even though it does not 'know' it is doing it. So, we can be quite certain that the rosebush, or any plant, doesn't have a self-aware I and doesn't know itself as a unique, one-of-a-kind, individual. You still have a way to go to reach that point where individual, personal, self-conscious I awareness showed up on Earth. It's time to move on.

* * *

* * *

Who am I?
What can I possibly be?

It's humbling to imagine that I
am the ultimate result of...
how many eons of
evolution?

I AM... all the way to ...I
So, let's get on with it!

* * *

Moving Like an Animal

Part One

Animals are incredibly more evolved than plants, just like plants are incredibly more evolved than rocks. However, in primitive species, individual slugs, worms, or insects are still not aware that they are individual slugs, worms, or insects. In fact, although they are physically separate from each other, they are not separate conscious beings.

Though they appear to be individuals from the outside, they share a common inner reality that defines the actions and activities of that species. As a result, they exist in group consciousness as opposed to individual consciousness, something originally defined by Rupert Sheldrake as a "Morphogenetic Field". Its main and guiding principle is ultimate survival, not of the individual, but of the species.

Army ants, for example, will move through the Brazilian jungle in an uncountable phalanx, miles long, inexplicably heading towards some unseen, undefined goal in the distance. Should they come to a body of water they do not stop but continue straight ahead. The first ants enter the water and drown, others climbing on their backs and drowning, the pile of dead ants building an underwater bridge until, at last, one ant makes it across, to be followed by the rest.

A group mind working for the good of the species makes much more sense than thinking that each ant has an individual consciousness and voluntarily commits suicide for the good of the group. I, personally, cannot conceive of any individual ant thinking, "Damn, just when I finally make it to the front of the line, wouldn't you know it, we're heading for a river."

New Consciousness would say that the army ant does not know it is going to die, first because the ant does not know itself as an individual physical entity, and second because the I of the group does not die with the individual. Such group minds, or morphogenetic fields, suggest that repeated activity of a particular kind by a particular species creates energy patterns that can be tapped into by others on the same wavelength.

This would be the same force that permits swallows to fly to Capistrano though they've never been there before, while giving migrating butterflies a different flight pattern and time schedule. It's what allows bees, without the aid of drafting tools, to create hives with perfectly hexagonal cells, and what permits a school of fish to turn on a dime.

Since such knowing exists in the group mind of a given bird, bee, butterfly, or fish, it can't be measured or weighed by biologists. However, such a concept doesn't dispute any of biology's external findings while giving a reasonable explanation for instinctive behavior. Further, it assuages humanity's fragile ego by explaining why a pea-brained bird can do something that a large brained person cannot. Even the simplest radio receiver can take in a lot of information if it's tuned into only one station.

New Consciousness resonates with the idea of such a morphogenetic field of inner consciousness and places the group-mind concept within the non-measurable inner reality of each species or subset. The individual bird or bee taps into that energy but doesn't have individual I awareness of doing so. The group consciousness functions as the motivating "instinctive" force for any given bird or bee as a common inner reality, a reservoir, so to speak, from which the individual bird or bee draws awareness before knowing individual I, the same as occurs on a less complicated level with plants.

New Consciousness also takes this idea one step further, suggesting that the energy field that is being tapped into by the bird and the bee is not just the wake of prior action, comparable to that left on the surface of a lake by a speedboat, but rather is the totality of shared consciousness, the mind of each species itself, prior to individuation. In other words, rather than there existing an individual mind for each separate physical entity tapping into waves, there's a single consciousness, a single mind, that exists for an entire species, physically outside the body of the individual, at least at lower evolutionary levels.

Much as a computer terminal collects and transmits data to a central processing unit where the actual computation takes place, so the primitive animal acts as a receiving station, collecting impulses from the surroundings through its senses, inputting them non-consciously into the species mind, which then sends back the impulses leading to appropriate action in that particular circumstance. The more primitive the species, the greater the effect of shared species mind on the animal, coupled with less individual differentiation and personality of the particular species member.

* * *

Part Two

It's a long way on the evolutionary continuum from the group mind of army ants and slugs to dogs, cats, gorillas, and other animals who clearly have individuation, uniqueness, personality, and individual consciousness. Somewhere in between lies the transition from group consciousness to individual consciousness, the experience of self as separate from the whole and the awareness that I am *in here* and something else is *out there*.

Could it be visual attraction to something I want to consume? Visual aversion to something that wants to consume me? That sounds pretty basic. But it could be even simpler. Imagine being a snake slithering along the ground. What do I experience as my skin begins to shed off? Do I even notice, and if I do, when is it no longer me?

Gradually, over eons, individual species started consciously experiencing outer reality, as we do with the world when waking after a long, deep sleep. Gradually, over eons, individuals within those species started consciously losing contact with inner group mind, as we do with our dreams when waking after a long deep sleep. Here is where you, sweeping in from the ends of time and space as pure undifferentiated consciousness, as I AM, will meet up with the first physical being to know of itself as alive and unique.

How does that first I know of itself as separate? How does it first experience a conscious, self-aware I? Is it a sound it hears and feels inside compared to a similar sound heard without the feeling of making that sound? Or a smell in the jungle never smelled before, a smell that is not-I? It could happen in so many ways. We know it involves the senses since the senses are what connects us to what is *out there* and lets us know that an *out-there* even exists. Does it matter how it happens? Isn't that just the content of knowing rather than knowing itself?

Such realization would not have been sudden for the species, a total group I becoming separated individual I for each member in an immediate, lightning-like swoop. Rather, it would have evolved as an element of the path we have been tracing all the way from rocks. Ever more evolved nervous systems, more sensitive sense organs, larger brains developed, physical beings ever more capable and aware of processing and responding on their own to inputs coming from outside, ever smarter terminals for consciousness, so to speak.

Meanwhile, back at the ranch, or jungle, or forest, or whatever external setting you'd like to imagine, you have been preparing for 'now' from the beginning of time, way back when you physically started to evolve, slowly at first, then ever faster, even as the changes became more and more complex, gaining physical capabilities to allow recognition of your presence, to allow recognition of consciousness.

Down you dive as non-material consciousness towards the initial meeting with your material non-aware self, heading toward Earth at the speed of knowing. The body you are aiming for is down there somewhere, waiting unknowing, prior to the first cognitive experience of self on Earth: the first individual I experience.

And there it is, the non-conscious being standing there, minding its own business, doing what it does, not knowing anything, not even knowing that it is. The mission is looking good, and in your mind, you feel almost like a voyeur.

You are closing in fast, perhaps too fast, but it's too late now to stop and brake. You will be entering its brain and experiencing this evolutionary moment of truth as it happens, the first Earthly awareness of I, from inside, from the inside of a physical, material being. You quickly scan the gauges. It's a go!

You know who you are—Universal Non-Material Consciousness. And you know that you are about to enter your Material Non-Conscious Creation, which will recognize your presence for the very first time.

Yes. Now. Non-Conscious Matter, experiencing nothing inside... nothing... nothing at all... until I get there.

...in its brain...
...inside...
...'now'...
...it is...
...I AM...

Touchdown!

"AAIIGGHH!!!"

A sound comes out of the creature's mouth. Translation...

"*What the... ?*"

You smile. With nothing to compare the feeling to, you should have known this is how a non-conscious being would first experience the I feeling, not as an awareness that I am or a thought-out understanding of self, but as a sudden reaction and feeling of something unknown.

Clearly, that being's very first awareness of I had to be of not knowing, not knowing what it is I have just become aware of since what has just happened is something I have never experienced before. Up to this point it's all been done on instinct, on autopilot. That's why the first awareness of self has to be "What the...?", not "Who am I?".

Interestingly enough, just before you got there is when that being's relation to the world outside is at its most efficient, where mind and body are one. Think of it. Where physical activity is concerned, the most efficient use of your mind is when it merges with your body. No extraneous thoughts, no musings, no asides, no "what ifs". Nothing separating you from what your physical body is experiencing at that moment, being in the here and now. At the very least, you are in tune with your environment. This perfect relationship between inside and outside is what we call instinct. And this is the shared characteristic of the simplest, most primal animals.

Animals do not know the name of a certain bush, or that something is even a bush, or that there are even such things as names. They do, however, go over and eat its bright red berries. And they do that without even thinking about it.

As it turns out, instinct and mental capacity are at opposite ends of the spectrum. The more evolved the species, the more developed the mind. The more developed the mind, the less the creature does by instinct. The dog is more evolved than a frog, which is more evolved than a slug. The more it can think, the less instinctive it is. That's why humans are destroying the very planet we live on, something less evolved beings would never do. But I digress.

You rise out of the creature's head, and it doesn't notice. You re-enter, and again it is startled by something now vaguely familiar. You squeeze in and settle behind its eyes, between its ears, quietly, silently, unobtrusively allowing it to experience the outer world through its senses. It...

there is something that it does not know. And though it won't be able to name it for eons, it now knows I am. Of course, it doesn't matter what kind of body you have entered. The perspectives of outer reality registered by the senses of each I will differ; some are in trees, some on the ground, some in water. But the inner worlds are similar.

Inner reality has been activated into awareness for the very first time and the creature is now looking inside as well as outside, consciously reacting to those inputs it is receiving from the outer world. It does not know it, but you do. Outside nothing has changed. Or has it?

It seems so obvious once one has experienced awareness of self and other. But the first time is incomprehensible when there is nothing to compare it to. So, too, is the revelation of no longer having to follow a single pre-programmed response to the inputs of the outer world.

Imagine a little creature running from its burrow to the water hole. Every day it is on the path, the same path, the beaten down path, the path from here to there, the path it has run every day of its life, the path its ancestors have run every day of their lives. It doesn't know what it is doing. It doesn't think about what it is doing. It just does it. It doesn't even know that it can know what it is doing, and that's the point. Imagine the feeling that very first time it stops in its tracks, and it hits...

I don't have to stay on this path! I can go this way, or I can go that way. I can choose which way to go. Talk about an altered state of consciousness!

As the material senses and inner realities of the beings evolve, each additional capacity allows a new way to experience outside, to differentiate I from not-I, and to recognize differences between others. It's very interesting. Not all senses speak the same truths.

The eyes are keen, yet they cannot always be trusted. What looks like a peaceful, safe haven can hold, within its unseen shadows, a hidden being who views me as the dinner that nature is so generously providing. Seeing is not always believing. I...

that, without even knowing I know it.

But listening is believing, for sound does not lie. The sounds of the outer world have no hidden meanings, never speak other than the obvious, and never tell other than the truth. The sound from above tells simply clearly and openly of the wind passing through the trees, nothing more, nothing less. The sound of water conveys nothing more nor less than the identifying presence of the waterfall, the running brook, and the melting icicle. The sound I make conveys nothing more nor less than the presence of me experiencing myself, experiencing I.

These sounds of the natural world reflect a set of linguistic laws known as Grice's Maxims, which holds that conciseness, relevance, clarity, and truthfulness are the rules of speech that would characterize human conversation if the transmission of factual information were the only purpose of that communication.

In our newly self-aware creature's "now", such direct, purely factual transmission is the norm. In today's "now", on the other hand, with the exception of direct military orders, rocket launches, and reruns of Dragnet, humans have distanced ourselves far from this natural, informational-focused speaking. We ramble on and on and on and on, and head off on tangents in all sorts of different directions, which may or may not relate to the original subject, while losing our audiences in a morass of sesquipedalian logorrhea.

Our self-aware creature makes sounds, just like all the others of its kind. The sound is the process, clear and self-identifying, since the sound came before it was even aware of making the sound, before knowing I made it, before knowing I. That's why, when you showed up, the response was so open and honest.

AAIIGGHH!!!

Clearly, the making of sound came before any attempt to communicate, since communication already requires the recognition of both I and other. After all, without such awareness, who would I be attempting to communicate with? No I. No other.

You fine-tune your focus. As an evolving I, our creature increasingly reflects and acts directly on input from outer reality. It is now giving that reality meaning on its own without sending that information out to the larger, more inclusive group mind for processing. It has its own memories and is processing itself what had been previously processed in the group mind.

Little by little, awareness develops, quantitatively in how much can be processed, qualitatively in what sorts of things can be processed, and experientially in how that processing is perceived. As this grows, there also grows a parallel reflection of self-awareness of the I that is having these perceptions. These steps do not take place at once.

Newly emerging I doesn't know that it isn't in group mind. It doesn't even know that group mind exists even though it used to be part of it. It simply wakes to an awareness that feels like self and is now related through the individual body.

It looks around at bushes heavy with berries and tasty things to eat and takes its fill of them, drinking all it wants from the nearby water hole. The temperature is just right and it feels safe and satisfied and at ease. There is nowhere to go, nothing to do, and nothing to think about, since there's nothing to think with even though an awareness of self is developing, something that came long before cognitive capabilities.

Time passes. Our evolving creature is learning to tell the difference between sounds. The cry of the birds warns of predators and the crackling sound of last year's fallen foliage makes it stop and freeze in its tracks. Is something there? Every sound is being associated with a meaning of its own and survival means knowing the meaning, though it does not have names to describe them, other than the sounds themselves.

Feeling safe, it stretches and lies back on the soft turf, settling down into the lush ground cover, eyes closing, aware of the various sounds as they fade into one. Everything is as it should be.

Suddenly, the silence is shattered by a shrill, piercing screech coming from the tops of the trees and resounds inside its head.

"*BRRRRRRAAAACK*"

Our creature is suddenly wide awake! It reacts by running up a tree, diving down a burrow, or swimming out into the middle of the lake—it's so hard to tell from here.

Yet you can share the feeling it is feeling. It's as if someone ran into a room where you are sleeping, yelling "FIRE!". You give meaning to the sound "FAH-YER", or you would simply be startled by the noise, roll over, and go back to sleep. Only because that sound in your outer world evokes an inner response from a previous 'now' and projects a potential into a future 'now' will you take evasive action. You would do what our creature just did.

Now, if you and I react because we ascribe meanings to sounds, then our little creature must be ascribing meanings to sounds if it reacts in the same way. And since meaning comes from an inner reality, it is obviously accessing both realities, comparing the immanent outer experience of the sound with the experience of a previous 'now' that can only be accessed inside.

Whether it knows it or not, our creature is developing an I, a stored individualized inner file parallel to its knowing of the outer world in which it lives. Processes are happening fast and furious since you showed up. The evolutionary process has come a long way.

Thinking Like a Human

Back in the bushes, a familiar predator is lurking. You tune into its inner reality just as it calls out in the voice of a different species, the sound of an 'other'.

...KOOO... ...KOOO... ...KOOO...

The predator hopes to fool some being into believing it has gone away and that all is safe. The predator has discovered it's a good way to get lunch.

The distinction between self and other is no longer an unknown once I'm aware of separating from my natural speech. When that happens, a new level of knowing has been reached. I'm *in here*. It's *out there*. I know what I mean. It does not. I know that I am pretending, falsifying outer reality so as to confuse another's inner meaning. I know I am doing this, while it does not. Is it any wonder that cannibals ate humans from different tribes who spoke different languages? They do not understand us. They are not one of us. They must be food.

And so, we have come full circle, we have returned to human. As the human who is reading these words, I know what being human feels like. I know about going in and going out, recognizing the varying forms of others outside of me and the varying processes of mind inside of me. This is the way that I am and although I certainly don't know everything about me, I do know that I exist as a separate and unique being. I...

...that I am.

In linear terms, I have evolved from everything that came before, housing in my body and mind every aspect of consciousness that ever previously existed. As a human, my particular level of consciousness has evolved from the earliest forms on Earth in evolutionary movements along continuums of capability and individuation, constantly adding new capacities never dreamed of by the levels that came before.

My inner reality isn't just knowing that I am a unique and separate being, but a process constantly in motion taking place inside, a process that may or may not show up in the material world. I can think. I can imagine. I can place visions inside which are not in front of my eyes. I can imagine what might be. I can remember what has been. I can apply inner meanings to outer sounds through language. I can take abstract ideas and work them through to their conclusion.

Indo-European mind has placed the dividing line between inner reality and outer reality at the skin level, the barrier that seems for most of us to separate me *in here* from you *out there*. We have seen that this need not be so.

There are many cultures where body individuality is a subset of a conception of self as one pole of a series of relationships defined by family, village, and role in the community. The familial self involves emotional connectedness and interdependence. The concept of I means one thing with father, another with aunt, another with peers, and another with outsiders. Is this just an alternative societal construction different from ours, or might it reflect an awareness of group mind which Western mind has lost? In either case, is this not an example of the fact that body boundary is not an absolute requirement for human consciousness?

Suddenly, someone goes running through your head. "Stop", you call out, "who are you?"

"I am Xxxxxxx," they answer, giving the name of their tribe.

Does it really make sense to posit that inside and outside are based only on what is in front or in back of our physical eyes, that I am only that to which I am physically connected? Are my fingernails me only until I cut them? When I eat food, at what point in the process does it become me?

Are we not also capable of looking at our innermost thoughts and feelings and recognizing that if I am looking at them, they are somehow separate from I? Do we not watch ourselves do things and wonder who is watching and who is being watched?

This is the basis of the 12-step system, removing addictive behavior patterns from one's inner reality and externalizing those behaviors where they can be seen for what they are, processes we call 'habit' that I can choose to keep or discard. Nothing has physically moved from inside the body to outside the body. Only our awareness has changed in what we think of as inside and what we think of as outside. The habit was inside; now it is outside. As we do that, we change what we think of and experience as I.

The borders of our inner and outer realities are variable and based on where we choose to put them. Throughout the evolution of consciousness, they have been changing. Now, at this stage of the process have I reached a level where I can experience both the personal I and the Universal I. And since I can do that, evolution is still occurring.

* * *

* * *

I started in darkness... unseeing... unknowing...
with pressure within yet unable to tell.
Was I alone or was there another?
I reached and held on... as I faced the unknown.

I evolved in new ways to respond to my setting...
new forms designed to house who I am.
I could feel as it happened... in all of my beings...
till it all was too much to run from afar.

I entered the forms in a new sort of manner...
trading knowing the whole for knowing the part.
And as I evolved... I finally forgot...
forgot I was the One that inhabited all.

But the trip is not over... the adventure continues...
destiny mandates I should know the One.
Not unknowing and blind... like the way that I started...
but brilliant and shining and completely aware.

The I inside me is the I inside all.

* * *

How about that?

* * *

On Beyond Human

Welcome back, my friend. You've come a long way on the path of human evolution simply by playing some games, doing some exercises, and opening yourself up to a potential reality you might never have even thought of before. Give yourself a hand and step back for a moment to check out where you've been and what you've already experienced and accomplished.

You have discovered that you are not the adjectives and filters that make you unique but the consciousness that exists within those adjectives and filters. And you've experienced that the very feeling of I am that exists within your filters is the same feeling of I AM that exists inside everyone's filters; not only everyone, but everything, everything that does, ever did, or ever will exist in the entire universe.

You've even used that knowledge to make several trips in time - one to visit yourself in a younger version of your current body and one to visit yourself in a series of bodies you used to live in back when Earth was not as old as it is today.

(By the way, if you didn't actually feel the consciousness of the rock, the rose, or any of the other incarnations when you went on your trip, don't blame yourself. It's not that commonplace to slip out of the I who you are in your present life in order to accept the I of another physical being the first time around. I have been doing this for over forty years now and can tell you, it does get easier with practice.)

So, well done. Stick with it. Now that you know where and how to look, you are in a position to head back to the edge of the universe and the very beginning of time. Since, at least from the perspective of New Consciousness, you are that very same I who started the whole thing.

There are several ways we could go. Retracing the circuitous route that got us here, moving step by step back through the human mind, language, the animal mind, self-awareness, species mind, plant awareness, rocks, light, feeling, experiencing all the points of evolution from here to there. However, there is a shortcut. But first, let's bring the scientists on board.

Part Four:

Universe and Creation

* * *

I AM is inside everything.
The universe spreads out around ME.
Waves of consciousness forming a vortex
returning and surrounding I AM.

I AM heading out in so many directions...
having so many different experiences.
Each experience ever more unique...
for each individual I.

Facing the outer world I AM has created...
Interacting with waves from countless directions...
Consciousness merging from different perspectives...
That's what creates the material world.

I AM is having cool experiences... looking for Myself.
Yet, I just relate to what I see out there...
Not to the inner source of energy that created it all.
Yet that is who I really am... Each individual I.

I am that I AM

I AM and the Quantum Connection

Quantum physics seems to have hit a wall both literally and figuratively as it heads to the ends of the universe. I refer to the Event Horizons surrounding Black Holes that have become a main focus as quantum physics seeks to explain reality. So strong and impenetrable is this boundary, that it acts as a barrier not only to measuring but even to understanding what is happening on the other side.

According to those in the know, many pressing questions, such as the reality of space/time, non-locality, and the existence of a primal singularity, could well be answered if we could only penetrate event horizons to allow examination of the black holes existing inside. Well, it turns out event horizons can be penetrated. However, it occurs by looking in a new and unexpected direction as opposed to the one that science has been focusing its attention on.

While black holes and event horizons seem strange and impenetrable *out there*, they are a familiar and intimate part of our daily lives *in here*. Although we don't normally think of them this way, there is a clear parallel between the event horizon existing at the boundary of black holes and the event horizon existing at the boundary of individuals.

I am speaking of the event horizon separating you and me: the experiential boundary that creates and defines each and every one of us. Even though New Consciousness posits that the I experience at the center of each of us is the same, the individual filters and adjectives surrounding that individual I are clearly different for each of us. Therefore, someone from the outside cannot know and exactly duplicate the experiential reality of each individual I, and as a result, just like event horizons surrounding black holes in space, our individual event horizons cannot be penetrated.

You may get very close. As a surgeon, you may get inside my body. As a psychologist, you may get inside my mind. In either case, I am "me", and you are "you", and you are still looking at me from outside my conscious identity. That is just what astrophysicists have experienced as they try to enter black holes at the ends of the universe.

In addition, the event horizon we experience at the individual level displays characteristics amazingly similar to the event horizon studied at the cosmic level.

The world outside an individual's event horizon can be measured. It is made up of tangible forms, objective facts and particles. Events are witnessed in space and time.

The world inside an individual's event horizon cannot be measured. It is made up of intangible non-forms, subjective meanings and waves. Events are witnessed in the here and now.

Could it be that this event horizon that defines our very being and with which we are all so familiar is not any different from the event horizon that quantum physicists are looking to enter at the far ends of the universe? The answer from the perspective of New Consciousness, incredible as it first appears, is definitely, "Yes".

Physicists are also speculating that some form of immeasurable "dark energy" may actually be the source of all that is, that everything can be reduced to intangibles alone. Well, that dark energy physicists are claiming was present at the start of the universe sounds an awful lot like the very same universal consciousness we each experience every day inside our own event horizon. New Consciousness, as it turns out, is corroborating the findings of quantum physics. Or, you could say, that quantum physics is corroborating the findings of New Consciousness. Same thing.

What makes this awareness especially exciting is that it's the physicists themselves, who have brought consciousness and phenomenology into the conversation. They have come up with a concept they call Quantum Bayesianism or QBism that suggests there is a split or boundary between the world in which an observer lives and that observer's perception of the world. It's not the simple way we thought it was, they say. Mind creates reality. Well, welcome to the world of phenomenology.

Just as quantum physics has advanced towards this meeting of science and religion by moving into previously uncharted waters, the same can be said about the phenomenological side of the equation. Human consciousness is far from static and is, in fact, more verb than noun. Over the eons, what we experience when we refer to ourselves as I, is constantly in flux, changing right behind our eyes. This is something we have already experienced in Part Three of the Handbook as we traced the evolution of consciousness from its earliest days to the present. And, as we have also discovered, it is now time for life on Earth to take another evolutionary leap, this time into New Consciousness.

This is not just a subject for academic analysis. It is a way to be, a way to act, a way to understand the world and Self, which actually adds a new dimension to being human. Most interestingly, nothing needs to change in our current world for this new awareness to take place. Only our view of that world must change, based on where we stand, where we look, and what we bring to our meeting with that world.

The key to entering an event horizon, it turns out, is not trying to penetrate it from the outside, but to experience it from the inside, the place where the mathematical calculations of quantum physics and the experiential realities of phenomenology are both fulfilled.

Once science recognizes the commonality of the I AM experience and learns how to use New Consciousness to navigate its levels, we will be connected to everything in the universe that shares I AM consciousness, namely everything! This adds a whole new dimension to scientific study and opens up so many potentials that had been closed, only because we didn't know where to set up shop and in which direction to look for the answers.

As we have already done, we can travel backwards in time to experientially trace the conscious evolution of life on Earth. By watching ourselves as we eliminate mental capacity from human existence, we have experienced the devolution of consciousness from human to animal to plant to rock and back again.

Similarly, as we are about to do, we can use the very same techniques to experience the I AM existing at the beginning of space/time and be there at the very beginning of self-aware consciousness: the ultimate contrast between total light and total dark. After all, both science and religion do agree that it all began with "Let there be light".

* * *

(Until now, I have not shared any of my personal New Consciousness experiences. I share one now only because it so clearly parallels the trip you are about to take. Was it a vision? A memory? A dream? An out of body experience? Does it matter what we call it? It just was.)

* * *

The Spaceship Experience

I am inside a spacesuit, floating in space, white noise in my head, peering through a plastic visor at star-spangled blackness. Although able to move my arms and legs inside the suit, I feel somewhat constricted and begin wriggling around in my form-fitting environment. Strangely, the suit that fits so closely in front seems loose in the back. I push backwards and pull my arms and legs from their confines. As I do, I discover that the rear of the suit opens into a long tube, and I begin scooting backwards on all fours. All I can see are the inner walls of the tube and a glimpse of stars through the visor of the spacesuit, now receding far into the distance.

Suddenly, and with a resounding bone-jarring thud, I reach the end of the tube and fall out backwards, down three feet or so onto the solid tile floor of a brightly lit room. It is a large circular room, painted white. In the center are large engines and power pods, separated from the circular walkway on which I now stand by a simple iron railing. The outer perimeter of the room consists of a wall of windows, each with a control panel beneath it and a circular opening beneath that, similar to the one I've just fallen out of. The feeling is of being on the flight deck of a flying saucer. I am alone and remain so throughout the entire experience.

Looking out the window, I see my spacesuit floating far off in the distance, attached to the ship I am now in by the tube I just crawled through. I look at the control panel and realize that when I was in the spacesuit, I thought I was in charge of its movements, but that the true control of what goes on *out there* is done *in here*, on the flight deck of the mother ship.

Then I see zillions of other suits floating in space, each one attached to the mother ship through its own tube and control panel. I know that inside each and every suit is a person who thinks they are all alone in space and in control of everything that happens, just as I thought until I left the safety of my protective suit and made it here to the main craft.

And then ZAP! I'm back in the spacesuit again. But now I carry the knowledge of what I have just experienced.

* * *

The goal of the Handbook, as you have discovered by now, is to foster understanding of New Consciousness, not by preaching or sermonizing but by allowing you, the individual reader, to experience New Consciousness for yourself. You are a living being, made live by the Oneness that exists within you as your very feeling of I am. And since New Consciousness posits that I AM existed long before Earth existed, you should be able to have that experience, too. What say we give it a try.

* * *

I Am in Space

Level One

Sit down in a comfortable position. Or stand if you prefer. Or lie down. It's not your body that matters from here on in, or even your mind. It's your sense of Self. Your very sense of existing. We're going back inside. Way inside.

Reestablish your sense of I. Take a quick survey of what is inside. Take a quick survey of what is outside. What is I? What is not-I? Where do you put that event horizon between the two? Wherever you put that boundary, create a bubble that defines me and surrounds me. A bubble that separates me *in here* from not-me *out there*, the same as it always does. Feel that bubble surrounding you.

Now be an astronaut, floating in the blackness of space and see that unique, isolating bubble surrounding you as Pixar would do it. The event horizon bubble is my spacesuit.

Look through that transparent space suit protecting the I *in here* from the dangerous not-I *out there*. Experience the feeling of being protected from the emptiness surrounding me by that spacesuit. Be *in here*. Safe *in here*. Now close your eyes and give it a try.

(Once again, I suggest that you relax, take your time, and rather than thinking about it, really try to feel the experience. If you are having a hard time, don't get upset with yourself. It does get easier with practice.)

* * *

Level Two

Now feel yourself out floating in space surrounded by your event horizon, the protective bubble separating me *in here* from everything else that is not me *out there*. Relax. Feel protected. Feel peaceful. Feel safe.

Now unzip the back of your protective bubble and flatten it out in front of you!

What? Are you crazy? How?

No, I'm not crazy, and you know how. Just like the way Earth is a three-dimensional sphere but there are maps of it drawn in two dimensions that are flat. Just like that, except you are floating inside the sphere as it opens behind you, flattens out in front of you, and floats away. See it happen that way with your inner I.

So, now here I am, floating out in space, surrounded by nothing, looking at my protective bubble - the one I've always been inside - as it flattens out and moves away right in front of my very I. Interesting. The side I'm looking at used to be inside the bubble, like the lining of a coat. The side away from me used to be outside. That's the side that came into contact with the world. I am on this side. Not-I is still *out there* all around me, same as always. Yet somehow, I still feel safe. I still feel at peace even though I am open to the universe on all sides.

As the flat screen that used to be my protective bubble floats away and gets smaller, observe it meet up with other flat images from other bubbles that have opened from a lot of other individuals. Like those TV ads that start with one picture and then turn into four pictures and then become eight until it fills the screen with so many pictures that they all blend into one. Just like that. So many bubbles. In fact, my own personal bubble is now lost within the vast array. Which one is mine again?

* * *

Level Three

So now there are two places I can be: Here, floating in space inside my event horizon bubble, or here, floating in space with my flattened event horizon bubble somewhere off in the distance. And since it is all happening in my mind, I can go back and forth between them, like when I was looking at that old photo of me as a child. Plus, it's worth noting that even though the feeling of being I remains the same, not-I appears 3D when the bubble surrounds me and 2D when it flattens out in the distance.

So here is a question: Am I existing in two different points in space/time at once or am I switching back and forth between them? Or is there even a difference?

* * *

2D... 3D... 4D...?

Here is another question related to quantum physics. If I can experience my normal 3D world *out there* as a 2D flat screen projection, as I did in the mind game I just played, might that not suggest that the world I normally experience as my usual 3D reality might actually be 4D? To put it another way, if I flatten a 4D universe, does it turn Into a 3D experiential shell?

Interestingly enough, a number of quantum physicists have posited that we live in a three-dimensional shell surrounding a four-dimensional black hole. Our universe is that shell. If this is true, it only stands to reason that we cannot hope to experience, as three-dimensional beings, what is going on inside a four-dimensional reality without becoming four-dimensional, at least in our minds. This would be like the square in Flatland* trying to understand the reality of the sphere while remaining a two-dimensional square. Let's not be that square.

The key Is being able to recognize and experience that your 4D I and your 3D I would appear to be different even though they are both projections of the same I AM. Obviously, they would have different levels of

---

* *Flatland: A Romance of Many Dimensions* by Edwin Abbott, (Seeley & Co. 1884). A satirical book describing a two-dimensional world and what happens when a three-dimensional figure shows up.

awareness since they exist in two different dimensional realities.

This is why there is an experiential difference between I consciousness as it exists when I am in my physical body, and I AM, which is God Consciousness, Dark Energy, Oneness, or whatever you want to call it. With practice and awareness that both realities exist, both can be experienced at the new evolutionary level.

Most interesting of all is that I am capable of being in both places at the same time, switching perspectives and dimensions back and forth, faster and faster, until the transition feels absolutely seamless. But then, of course, even though I know that from the perspective of New Consciousness, the same I AM is actually within us all, I cannot forget that I am not-I to every other I. We are both One and separate, depending on how we look at it. How cool is that?

By the way, do not be upset if all this experiential theorizing doesn't just fall instantly into place for you. The moving of one's event horizon inward, inside the physical to where thoughts appear external, is an evolutionary step towards experiencing the ultimate 4D reality within. It does take time and practice. The goal is to go so far inside that everything is outside, even thoughts of who I AM. Ultimately, of course, when I can do that, it will take me back to the very beginning of it all.

* * *

* * *

Silken banner,
    matter hanging motionless,
        It does not move. Can you feel it?
        I think I can. Are you sure?
            There is nothing to feel with.

Invisible wind,
    energy through emptiness,
        It does not rest. Can you feel it?
        I think I can. Are you sure?
            There is nothing to be felt.

Without the power of wind, silk does not move. Without the resistance of silk, wind knows not its power.

Yet let moving energy meet motionless matter and play across its surface and there is life, made live by the interaction of wind and silk together.

They need each other... just to be. To be aware they are alive.

* * *

The Wind/Silk Experience

We, observing from a distance, know that both wind and silk exist. But wind and silk do not know. Without the power of wind, silk does not move. Without the resistance of silk, wind's power is unrecognized. They need each other for their own self-awareness.

Complementary polarities requiring each other for fulfillment are each valid because of the existence of the other. One is not good, and the other bad. One is not true, and the other false. They are simply two ways of knowing, filtered through the variable of individual awareness. Movement experiencing resistance; resistance experiencing movement. Male experiencing female? Female experiencing male?

Attitudes, feelings, understandings, behaviors, likes, dislikes, whole ways of being, of viewing and experiencing reality, strung deep within the experiencing individual, spinal even to cognition. Every thought and feeling built on a primal set, built on the experience of different and unique original ways of knowing I am.

There is no possible recognition of I unless there is an equally developed recognition of other, of 'apparent not-I'. Knowing of self implies knowing of non-self. I am. You are. Both can be realized at once. Both can only be realized at once.

* * *

I AM at the Start of The Universe

It is now time to go back to the very beginning and be there as the universe comes into existence - not by measuring from a distance in time and space, as science is attempting to do, but by experiencing it as it is happening in the ever-present here and now. New Consciousness allows you to do that from a perspective you have already experienced and accepted: non-physical awareness, God, dark energy, consciousness ... whatever you want to call it. We'll go from there.

* * *

Level One

You will be going back to before the birth of the universe. Prepare for the journey as you have done before for shorter trips. Get comfortable, turn off electronics, renew your awareness of inside/outside. Empty your mind of everything that couldn't have been there then - stars, planets, galaxies, space, time. Don't think about anything. Don't even think about consciousness. Just *feel* consciousness. Experience it.

And be aware that even though such Oneness can be experienced, it cannot be looked at while it is being experienced. Why? Because to look at something, you have to be outside of it. Or, conversely, it has to be outside of you. Even the ultimate samadhi, nirvana, and ecstasy of the great mystics, swamis, saints, and gurus are not capable of description by the very masters who have made it to the center of what we are now attempting to reach. Yet, even though you cannot see yourself while you are there, you can come back and feel the energy and know you've been there.

Five thousand years ago, the ancient people of the Indus Valley believed that true joy was the nature of God and the Ultimate Source of all that is. And since joy was the absolute ground of being and everything that exists in the universe, it was also the deepest purest part of our very nature as human beings. They named their God "Satchitánanda", a combination of three Sanskrit words: Sat - existence, Chit - consciousness, Ananda - bliss. Existence-Consciousness-Bliss. Or, as I like to think of it: "I am. I know that I am. Wow!"

In lives that followed more closely the simple rhythmic cycles, the flow of the seasons, the light of day, the dark of night, the ebb and flow of warm and cold and rainy and dry, it was easy to feel the larger patterns of Nature. Even though these early people did not know what we now know about the universe in any scientifically provable sort of way, they could look up into the clear heavens and panoply of stars, unhidden by smog and light pollution, and feel the joy of simply being connected to what they saw. And when they did, they knew this joy they felt within themselves was at the very heart of the universe as well.

It is much harder for modern humans to experience the pure joy of existence because we have not been living such simplistic lives. We've been looking for joy in all the wrong places, finding it sadly lacking in the things we buy, the things we own, the things we do, and oftentimes even the people we love. We have been looking for joy *out there*. All the advances in technology and pressures of day-to-day living that have occurred since the Indus Valley have put barriers between ourselves and the ultimate source of joy that exists at our very core.

So, relax. Turn off your mind. Feel I AM. What does it feel like? You already know that. Yes. Yes. I AM, and I know that I am. I AM THAT I AM. And at the start of it all, I AM is all there is. Now, put down this book, disappear into that feeling of pure existence, and stay there for as long as you can.

* * *

Welcome back. Can you see the importance of what you have just done? What you have just experienced? From now on, whenever you feel the pressures of the world closing in on you, you can take some time to go inside, deep inside the adjectives that define you to the place within where you feel the I AM at your very core. Don't think about it. Feel it. The pure joy of just plain being, of just plain existing. What were the chances? And yet you made it. Way to go. Feel the Joy. You are I AM. Wow!!!

Congratulations on what you have just accomplished. No matter how deep you have gone, no matter how long you have stayed there, even for an instant, if at any point you lost track of the physical being doing the experiment and became the joy, you have touched that point of Oneness that resides within us all. And now, having experienced absolute Oneness, in all that joy, it is time to experience the birth of the Universe.

* * *

Level Two

Be here floating in nothingness, in darkness, in blackness, complete blackness, total blackness. What am I looking at? What can I be looking at? There is nothing to see. What am I thinking about? What can I be thinking about? There is nothing to think about? Nothing to see, nothing to visualize, nothing to focus on, nothing to know. No time. No space. No *out there* to look at. No *in here* to remember. There is nothing - no-thing. All that exists is the experiencing of I AM. Feel I AM, for that is all that is. And know that I AM can become anything I want.

Science has recently started positing that rather than some Big Bang where an improbably dense singularity exploded and created our universe, we are actually a three-dimensional shell surrounding an imploded four-dimensional universe. Thought waves slowing down and manifesting into particles. I AM creating light and the ability to turn around and look at Itself. To be whatever I want to be. This could explain why nothing in space/time existed before the Big Bang. This was the first idea I AM had.

Just as nothing humankind has ever produced was not first visualized in a person's mind before it appeared in physical reality, the universe didn't exist before it did simply because I AM had never thought about it before.

Religion has long said the universe began with "Let there be light". A light in the darkness, more than just the ability to see, the ability to know, to know who I AM. Total light contrasting total darkness. Mental waves contrasting physical particles. The first idea come to light. Why do cartoon characters get an idea by having a lightbulb go off in their mind?

Let there be light!

Ancient civilizations and philosophies have been saying for millennia that I AM is the origin of it all. The ancient teachings of Kashmir Shaivism, the I AM THAT I AM of The Bible, the modern philosophy of Sri Aurobindo, the "I am is the way" of Jesus, just to name a few.

The problem is that up until now, these have not been able to be tied down by mathematics and have been labeled merely religion and belief systems, both of which are antithetical to scientists.

How exciting to discover that due to quantum physics, these two supposedly diametrically opposed thought systems seem to be in agreement. Oneness, that has been presumed to be *out there* is really *in here,* inside each and every one of us. Think about it. What if the experience the ancients had was actually correct, and that now, because of the findings of modern quantum physics and neuroscience, their subjectivity could now become objective? That would be big.

Just as I am blind in total darkness, so am I blind in total light. Try visualizing seeing something in total blackness. Solid black. Nothing but black. Can you do it without visualizing some flashes of light for contrast? Holes in the solid black? Try it. No. It can't be done. Try visualizing total light. Bright light. Nothing but light. Can you do it without visualizing some flashes of black for contrast? Holes in the solid light? Try it. No. It can't be done.

This is why some physicists are now saying that shortly after the initial flash created the universe, all went dark for a short period of time. Yes. Makes sense. I AM would have experienced two extremes but still needed to improve the design of what was being imagined and, thereby, being created.

And so, I come back, little by little, new stars coming into being. Holes in the darkness. Playing with it. Trying different things I can do, different things I can be. Experiences I can have. Growing, evolving, expanding, contracting, intersecting and becoming ever more complex. I am constantly creating a more and more material reality farther and farther along from where I started. Farther *out there* in a lesser dimension.

* * *

Level Three

Be the fire in the star. Be the waves of consciousness moving farther and farther away from the aware creative center. Cool. Form a crust. Feel it. *Out there*, outside of ME. More and more complex. I AM expanding into separate beings. I am ever expanding housings to hold my very own consciousness. More and more physical, more and more material, until at last, my creations forget who they really are.

Over the eons of materialized time, I AM complexifying my shell to the point of reaching a limit of solid, material, non-conscious particles in absolute contrast to the non-material, self-aware waves that started it all. At one end of the spectrum: non-material consciousness. At the other end of the spectrum: non-conscious materiality. Different beings evolving to different levels, experiencing wave and particle to different degrees. Reality is the total spectrum, with you and I and every creature in the universe living in between and experiencing them both; wave and particle, inside and outside.

Does I AM try things that don't work, can't go on, that run out of energy? Bad designs, so to speak? Of course. They implode. From the outside: a black hole. From the inside: better luck next time. Perhaps humans fall into this category. Who knows? We're still working on it. In any case, I AM still exists. And there are so many possibilities I AM can become, one of which is you, the I reading these words on planet Earth in a 3D universe.

Inner waves of consciousness are creating ever more complex physical realities. The outer material world is limited to space/time. The inner world is unlimited. The conscious I experience remains the boundary between inside and outside. I = outside x inside^2?

Our 4D I and our 3D I are not the same. They have different capacities since they exist in two different dimensional realities. I AM exists in 4D as well as 3D. Physical I am is limited to experiencing only through my 3D shell.

From the end of space, from the start of time, only now (at least in this part of the universe) am I able to produce a self-reflexive 3D shell (human) capable of housing a 4D understanding (human+) of the grandeur, the humor, and the mathematics of it all.

"I AM THAT I AM"
inside each and every one of us...
and One with everything.

* * *

Quantum Physics and Phenomenology

Phenomenology has been defined as the philosophical study of the structures of experience and consciousness. Its goal is to describe any phenomenon through the actual lived experience of the experiencer. What I bring to the table, in a diner or in my expectations of what might exist at the ends of the universe, cannot help but affect what I will find and what my experience will be.

Quantum physicists are beginning to recognize that this phenomenological approach is not just limited to philosophers. Reality is not just a case, as Newtonian physics once thought, of simply looking out there and measuring what you see. It is more a case of looking out there and creating the level and depth of the very things we are looking at. The observer does affect that which is observed. Where we look and what we are looking for can affect what we find and where we find it. And as a result, we have a real and actual role in the creation of the universe around us.

This finding of modern quantum physics is completely in agreement with New Consciousness. As scientists learn to work with phenomenology, numerous experiential findings will be discovered which are in agreement with and/or explain specific theories currently posited by quantum physics. Here are a few. Since they fall beyond the scope of the Handbook and its goal of helping us find and experience New Consciousness, there is no need for readers to delve into them in depth unless you are a quantum physicist or just really want to do so. I list them here solely for the pure fun of doing so and previewing where evolving consciousness can lead us.

* * *

1. **Consciousness, the very feeling that I AM, is the Oneness that fills the Universe.**

Religion calls it God. Science calls it Dark Matter/Energy. Same thing. It exists both within and without everything in space/time.

2. **Consciousness is the experiential synapse between Inside and Outside.**

I can only experience myself *in here* if I can experience a 'not-self' *out there*. No dark without light, no light without dark. This is why there is no physical space/time before duality.

3. **Consciousness equals the speed of light squared.** $C = c^2$.

The material universe is created when consciousness sloughs off some of its infinite possibilities (waves), manifesting particular conceptual potentials (particles) while slowing to the speed of light, thereby creating time.

4. *Evolution is the constant creation of ever more complex housing for consciousness.*

On one end of the spectrum is non-material consciousness. On the other end of the spectrum is non-conscious materiality. I exist in-between and experience both inner wave and outer particle, whatever my level of conscious awareness.

5. *Individual conscious awareness equals energy over matter. C = e/m.*

Matter in space/time is not conscious but a 'housing' for conscious energy. From star to human, a being's awareness of its own consciousness is related to its ratio of energy to matter.

6. *Event horizons surround all creations in space/time where individual conceptual assumptions are not consistent with absolute, universal, I AM consciousness.*

Individual space/time assumptions produce limited I consciousness that is impenetrable from the outside. This is true for humans as well as stars and galaxies.

7. *Black holes can be examined, but only from within a shared event horizon.*

By removing our own individual space/time assumptions, we can experientially return to points of inner commonality and go forward from the point of deviation using the assumptions of the black hole being examined.

* * *

Yes. I create the universe. From the very beginning to the present moment. Know it. Feel it. Be it. Each I am an I AM of its own, not a particle but a wave and a particle. I AM wave. I am particle. Hardening shells falling off the wave and becoming matter as along the way I lose my sense of connectedness to the origin and relate only to my shell even though I truly connect with both.

Evolution, from the end of the universe, from the start of time. Consciousness slowing to the speed of light in order to exist in three dimensions. And now, in this manifestation of thought existing in the material, is I AM able to produce a creature capable of housing an understanding of the grandeur, the magnificence, and the humor of it all.

I AM THAT I AM inside each and every one of us. Go ahead. Say it. I am. You've been saying it your whole life. What's different? Now, it means something more.

I AM

* * *

* * *

I stand between darkness and light...
between matter and energy.
I am what connects them.
At the speed of light squared.

Energy comes through me
light sprays patterns...
on the darkness of my mind.
So many possibilities.

Spray enough patterns
and possibilities manifest
Into three-dimensional time and
So solid matter.

* * *

Putting It All Together

Thank you, my friend, for making it through the Handbook from one end to the other. I wasn't sure you would make it all the way. A lot of folks who start out on the journey don't end up here. So, give yourself a pat on the back. You've earned it.

It's not easy staying on track, looking for the Jewel of Truth and adding it to your life when there are so many other things that can get in your way. Things like making a living, or watching tv, or preconceived notions, or prior beliefs.

Yes, I understand. New Consciousness is certainly a lot to take in. Especially since it's not something to just read and put down but something meant to become a part of you from here on in. How can you learn who you are at your very core and not be somewhat awed at the grandeur of it all? How can you learn who everyone else is at their very core and not treat them with love and respect?

As said at the very beginning, it's not as if this hasn't been said before, at different times, or in different ways. How many sages? How many masters? How many prophets? How many gurus? Each one has said it slightly differently, and we humans tend to focus on the differences rather than the similarities. So rather than celebrating what we share in common and growing from what we can learn from our differences, we magnify the differences and shut our ears to what others have to teach. We are not all the same. Why, then, should the way we have been enabled to see the truth be the same?

You are a unique manifestation of the Absolute, and your understanding of that truth will be unique as well. Yes, you should listen to what others wish to share with you, and yes, if you wish, you can share what you know with others as well. But you must never forget: there are many ways to discover the truth, and the only person who is wrong is the one who says, "My way is the only way".

The Handbook has tried not to simply preach and tell you how I think things are, but to help lead you to the point where you can find out how things are for yourself. Using games and experiences and self-reflection you've discovered a lot. You've discovered how to know what you know so you can trust your own experiential truths. And that starts with knowing the universality of the consciousness you feel within as your very being.

You've learned that words can mislead and that the language a person uses absolutely colors the way they think and what they believe. And, speaking of words, you've learned that names do not matter when it comes to what you call the Truth.

You have discovered that your very sense of being requires a constantly changing focus between inside and out, between who you are and who you are not. One side gives measurement, one side gives meaning. To be a functioning individual, you must relate to both.

You have learned to recognize the relativity of experience: that what is true for you may not be true for me and yet we can both be right. Using your inner I, you've traveled in time, going back to the past to share the experience of your younger self. And you've realized that you can visualize your future and by so doing, affect what will materialize in the world yet to be, just as was done at the beginning of space/time. And, hopefully, along the way, you've met your higher self, your own inner *The Elder*, whatever name you wish to use.

You've seen the parallels between science and religion, and even though they use different words and describe different perspectives, they are both really espousing the same thing. A singular energy, being, whatever you want to call it, that was here at the beginning and is still here today. And you've traveled back to the start of life on Earth and discovered how that singular energy was experienced by different life forms all along the way.

Finally, you've ridden that energy all the way back to the beginning of time and space to feel how it all began, using nothing more than the same abilities you already have, only viewed from a different platform. And no matter how vivid your experiences are, and they will get more vivid with practice, there is no question that you've accomplished a lot. If you're exhausted, I don't blame you.

Most importantly, you have learned a way of being that, when put into practice, can clearly improve your personal life experience.

When the reckless driver cuts you off on the highway, or your inconsiderate neighbor mows down your flowers while working on their lawn, or that family member (you know who I mean) acts up again at a family gathering, you can take a moment to realize that at your core you are peace, love, and joy - and you don't have to react. What's done is done and negative emotions will neither improve the situation nor the way you feel.

When you live in New Consciousness you realize that hurting another is hurting yourself. By looking at other people not as separate from my Self but rather as different versions of my Self, you just might find yourself more forgiving, more tolerant, and more loving. Love them as you love yourself.

Other people are going through their own set of problems, conflicts, and learning experiences the same as you are and your peace and calmness in facing the day-to-day problems of the world may not only ease their situation, it can set a positive example for others without you having to say a word.

There is an old Chinese proverb that goes something like this:

* * *

A peaceful man makes a peaceful household.
A peaceful household makes a peaceful neighborhood.
A peaceful neighborhood makes a peaceful village.
A peaceful village makes a peaceful state.
A peaceful state makes a peaceful country.
A peaceful country makes a peaceful world.

And it can all start with me.

* * *

As a very intelligent friend of mine recently said, "When I fully accept myself exactly as I am, so do I do the same with others. What greater impetus or reason does one need to act from loving kindness in all one does?"

And as a bonus, there will come a day as it does for all of us, be we humans or trees or stars or galaxies, when our physical manifestation ceases, and our consciousness returns to its source. At that time, no matter how New Consciousness manifests in your life from this point on, the information you took in through the Handbook will prove of value, for you will remember what you read here when you need it most. You will see the light and feel the energy and though you may not want to leave your body and the ones you love, you will know that you are not that body, and there is nothing to fear. And when that time comes, what you have experienced here will be a blessing.

In conclusion, despite all my years of work and all my good intentions, I know that the Handbook is not the final word on consciousness, human evolution, or the future of life on Earth. However, I trust that it is a step forward that could raise individual awareness and ultimately help humanity shift to a path that would cause less pain and suffering than the path we are currently on.

I know there are scientists who resonate with what is written here. I humbly offer you my life's work. How do my experiments in consciousness fit in with your theories, your numbers, your life's work? How might we work together to answer the basic questions about the universe and help take human knowledge to the next level of evolution? You'll have to do the math. I can only tell you what it feels like.

I know there are religious leaders out there who also resonate with what is written here. I humbly offer you my life's work as well. Knowing that the One is within us all, let us put aside sectarianism and open ourselves and those who trust our voices to the acceptance of different paths. Let us eliminate the fear of differences and teach that by seeing I to I we become the best I can be and the One we truly are.

Finally, I know that each and every individual has the ability to change the world. We may not be able to stop wars on the other side of the globe or feed every being who goes to sleep hungry, or end all the hate and injustice caused by prejudice and ignorance. But we can affect the world around us. We can have a positive effect on those with whom we come into contact and, by so doing, make our little corner of the world a better place.

And when enough of us do that, when enough of us realize we are all connected and that hurting another is hurting ourselves, then humanity will have evolved and the world will be a better place for all - just as it was intended from the very beginning.

Thank you, my friend, for helping humanity evolve.

* * *

*Yes... my friend... you are I AM.
And so is everyone else.*

*God... Universal Consciousness...The One... The Self...
Dark Energy... The Void... All That Is... The Tao... I AM...
Satchitānanda... Brahma... Allah... Jahweh... The Big
Kahuna... The Cosmic Muffin... Grand Unification
Theory... and even The Jewel of Truth.*

*Just think what we can do
when we work together
as the One we truly are.*

* * *

Acknowledgments

One of the very keys to New Consciousness is the awareness that we are all connected and that, ultimately, nothing is actually done by one's self. This is certainly true for *Handbook for a New Consciousness* which would never have made it this far without widespread support of those who helped to get it published and distributed.

Before that, were the teachers and gurus whose lessons illuminated the mind of the author, creating something worthy of being said. These include those whom I met face to face, particularly Dr. Jim Ryan and Dan 'Moonhawk' Alford, from the California Institute of Integral Studies, as well as Sogyal Rinpoche, Baba Muktananda, and the Dalai Lama. There are also those who had long left their bodies but whose teachings still moved my soul, specifically Lahiri Mahasaya, Paramahansa Yogananda, Sri Ramkrishna, Sri Aurobindo, Dr. Haridas Chaudhuri, Lao Tzu, and Jesus of Nazareth. And, of course, there is *The Elder*, who never had a body to begin with.

Then there is family: my sister, Julie, who first introduced me to spirituality and has served for years as advisor, editor, and active critic, my wife, Phyllis, and children, Gerry and Dani. Living with and putting up with a motivated philosopher was probably not what you expected when you signed on. Thank you for your patience in putting up with my spouting and re-spouting of truths and beliefs I was attempting to make visceral. Thanks to my parents, Eugene and Marion, for giving me the skills and talents to put it all together.

And finally, I'd like to acknowledge my grandfather, George, who would have fought me tooth and nail over my belief in God, but whose dream of a world of Perpetual Peace and Universal Understanding, which I learned of on his knee, has been spinal for me my entire life. May *Handbook for a New Consciousness* help bring his dream to fruition.

About the Author

Anton Grosz has a PhD from the California Institute of Integral Studies in the Evolution of Human Consciousness and is a practitioner of phenomenology - the science of experiential reality. He is an ordained Interfaith Minister, a retired Hospice Chaplain, and a certified Home Care Provider. Born into a profoundly atheistic family, he denied anything religious for the first half of his life. In 1978, at the age of 37, he discovered spirituality through a Near Death Experience, going through a tunnel into the light and experiencing a multi-dimensional reality different and greater than anything he had ever thought possible.

Since then, he has devoted his life to studying different spiritual paths and teachings, leading meditation practice, and helping those at the end of life. He has also journaled and written about his numerous spiritual experiences and insights. His first book, *Letters to a Dying Friend: What Comes Next*, (Quest, 1989) has an introduction by the Dalai Lama, and his second book, *How Do I Live When I Know I'm Going To Die?*, (FMA Books, 2001), was distributed through the National Hospice and Palliative Care Organization.

Anton and his wife of 61 years, Phyllis, recently moved from San Francisco to Newark, Delaware. They have two adult children and two grandchildren.

He can be reached at - www.AntonGrosz.com.

www.ingramcontent.com/pod-product-compliance
Lightning Source LLC
Chambersburg PA
CBHW071909290426
44110CB00013B/1340